LRG Nation
Stories of Courage, Growth, & Belonging

Book 1

Marya Patrice Sherron

Edited by

John Vataha

Foreword by

Erin O'Mara Kunz

KI
PRODUCTIONS

KI Productions & Publishing
Noblesville, IN

To Kc...

My first lens reframed and where it all began.

Thank you, Friend.

Contents

Foreword   ix
Preface   xi
A Little LRG History   xiii

Part One
Belonging Begins with Courage

1. ALICIA GARZA   3
2025

2. CARLOS KIDDO   11
2024

3. BRITTANY J.   19
2024

4. ZACH FIFER   31
2024

5. ALYSON FOISY   39
2025

6. RACHEL ROWE   47
2026

7. ALLEN YANNONE   57
2024

Words of Wisdom   65

Part Two
Community Is Built with Intention

8. JOHN VATAHA   71
2024

9. NIKKI NEISES   79
2024

10. KC WINNECKE   87
2024

11. SHAW ASHLEY   93
2024

12. SANDRA DIAZ-TWINE   101
2024

13. MAE MESSERSMITH   109
2024

14. CHRIS LORD   115
2025

15. NAOMI C.   123
2026

Words of Wisdom   131

Part Three
Growth Requires Friction

16. MIRA HALL   137
2024

17. DEJUAN WATTS   145
2025

18. DANIEL SUCKOW   153
2026

19. JAYMES LANOYE   159
2026

20. RENZO SANTOS   169
2026

21. KADIE YANNONE   177
2026

22. DA'VONTAE RANDOLPH   185
2024

Words of Wisdom   193

Part Four
Staying Is a Choice

23. AMOS RAY SMITH   199
2024

24. KEENAN LUCAS   207
2026

25. FRANCES DIEDERICH   215
2024

26. JACOB BURKLOW-ROGERS   223
2024

27. ERIC ELDREDGE   231
2024

28. MELANIE BARTLETT   237
2024

Words of Wisdom   243

Part Five
Beyond the Game

29. STEPHEN STEWART   249
2024

30. ANGELA L. MILLER   257
2026

31. DANNY VOGWILL   267
2024

32. ERIN O'MARA KUNZ   275
2026

Afterword   285
Meet the Nation's Contributors   289
Acknowledgments   305
About the Author   307

FOREWORD

It started with a game.

People from all walks of life came together over their shared love for a game, ultimately forming the Live Reality Game (LRG) community. When this happens, it's easy to focus on the 'what'—the game itself. But that's not what Marya Sherron has done in *LRG Nation*; she looked beyond the game, beyond where others would have stopped, to focus instead on the people and the stories that were waiting to be told.

In *LRG Nation*, Marya Sherron shares stories she felt essential to tell —as if leaving them untold would be a loss to the community. Each chapter is written through Marya's unique, artfully positioned lens–one that sees what others would easily miss. She pushes beyond the surface, deep into the core of a person. She is uniquely skilled at weaving together the disparate threads of a person's life into a narrative that is both seamless and profoundly real. Marya appreciates the inherent complexity that lies within each person; she doesn't try to simplify complexity, she celebrates it.

My two decades as a social psychologist have taught me that the 'why' is almost always more interesting than the 'what.' Having spent my career analyzing human social behavior, I'm instinctively drawn to the psychological processes that drive the 'whys' and that is what made me appreciate *LRG Nation* so deeply. Marya looks past the "super-fan" stereotypes to unveil the way LRGs satisfy fundamental human needs, like the drive for competence, the search for purpose, and the unrelenting need to belong.

I felt a wide range of emotions while reading this book. Though I am relatively new to LRGs, my journey has been tumultuous and my own 'why' has evolved over time—moving from "this is the closest I'll get to playing the real *Survivor*", to something much more. This is echoed in Marya's writing, as the 'whys' are often completely untethered to the show that inspired them. For some, it's a form of self-validation or a way to satisfy their competitive fire. For others, games provide a sense of belonging, hope, and even devastation. The truth is that these games can gut you as quickly as they can elevate you, and *LRG Nation* doesn't shy away from that tough reality; it honors it.

As I reflected on *LRG Nation* and the incredible opportunity that Marya has given me—both by featuring my story and asking me to write this foreword—I realized that I was learning as much about Marya as I was the people in each chapter, myself included. She does something that not many authors have the courage to do: she turns her lens inward. Through the 'My Lens Reframed' sections, she transforms the book from a one-way observation into a living dialogue, sharing how she was personally altered by each exchange.

What I carry from Marya is the reminder that some of the most important stories sit back, quietly waiting to be discovered. If stories remain untold for a time, it is not because they are unimportant—it is simply because they are waiting for the right person to hear them. Marya was that person for us.

It started with a game. But it is, and has always been, about the people.

~ Erin O'Mara Kunz, Ph.D.

PREFACE
LOOK AGAIN: BEAUTY IN THE HUMAN SPIRIT

This book asks for a second look.

The conversations that shape *LRG Nation* took place between the fall of 2024 and February of 2026, across seasons of play, pause, and becoming. That span matters because lives do not stay still long enough to be documented cleanly. Games end. Roles shift. Certainties fracture. Some of the people you will meet here have since stepped into lives that did not yet exist when we spoke. What follows is not a final accounting. It is a moment held deliberately.

What lives here could never be captured by transcription alone. This book is not a record of events, but a series of portraits... each chapter told through my perspective, shaped by what lingered, what resisted easy language, and what stayed with me after the conversation ended. Every interview altered my understanding, not only of the game, but of identity, belonging, ambition, fear, and courage. Those experiences live inside the structure of each chapter, particularly in *My Lens Reframed*, and the closing reflections. They are not commentary. They are part of the work.

I am drawn to beauty... not the polished kind, but the human kind. The kind that appears in contradiction. I attend to what is spoken, and I listen for what hovers just beneath it: the pause before an answer, the humor that deflects, the silence that carries weight. Often, the truest story does not announce itself. It waits in the silence to be discovered. *To be seen.*

One interviewee was initially concerned that I had made them seem "perfect." I hadn't. Perfection has never interested me. What I offered was a composition... a deliberate *choosing*. Not of what to erase, but of what to hold in the light. Strength beside uncertainty. Resilience braided with fragility. Not a pedestal, but a portrait.

The sketches that anchor each chapter are not autobiographical records. They are interpretive acts. They are how I choose to see and hear and understand the human heart. In sketching, I am not attempting to capture everything; I am zooming in on what feels essential. Selection, here, is not omission—it is intention. Each sketch is an argument for attention, a refusal to flatten complexity into spectacle or flaw-hunting. This is not about making people exemplary. It is about making humanity visible.

Their stories required something of me.

Listening with this level of care demanded that I kept the lens outward and simultaneously, willing to turn it inward. As I sought a deeper understanding of myself, I began questioning my motivations, my choices, the quiet desires that guide my work. Who is Marya? What am I building and what am I avoiding? Am I living... leaving a legacy?

Some of the answers unsettled me. I did not like everything I found when I stopped editing myself for comfort and finally told the truth.

The sketches became my response.

They were a deliberate choice to look for what repairs rather than what diminishes, to leave things better than I found them, to practice a way of seeing that insists on care without denial. In the end, this was not only how I told their stories... *it was how I learned to live my own.*

These are their stories as I encountered them, as they challenged me, and as they asked something of me.

Through my lens.

Reframed.

A Little LRG History

By Stephen Stewart

When *Survivor* premiered in May 2000, it was an immediate sensation. Around 52 million viewers watched the *Survivor: Borneo* finale to see who the first sole survivor would be. The microcosm of society that the show captured, the survival aspect on the island, the slice of life of the contestants, the strategy – all of these drew people to watch it. That season and every season since then, the show has put out a casting call, asking viewers to get off the couch and go on an adventure of a lifetime. Each year, thousands answer that call, with a lucky 40 or so people selected to embark on that journey.

Something *Survivor* perhaps never anticipated though were the people that watched the show and thought to themselves, *I can make a game like that too.* Or the people who watched, applied, didn't get cast, yet still itched at a chance to prove to themselves that they could survive the elements and the other players. Many reality TV shows that have premiered since then, from *Big Brother* to *The Mole* to *The Traitors*, have fostered a similar desire in its viewers. All of this has led to fans stepping up and creating their own games for other fans to play. All of this led to the birth of *Live Reality Games* (LRGs).

Of course, these games weren't always known as LRGs. That term can be first traced back to players from a game in 2015, *Pirate Booty*

Camp. The term itself can be seen as a distinction from *Online Reality Games* (ORGs), which are reality TV style games played online through chat or video features. LRGs are different in that they require players to meet up in the same physical environment.

As to when the first of what we now know as LRGs occurred, that's hard to pin down. For a *Survivor*-inspired game, was the first game played after the *Survivor: Borneo* premiere, finale, or sometime later in the future? There is no definitive evidence for what could be the first LRG that was ever created. Given what we know of how most games start, early LRGs were perhaps one or two-day competitions put on by friends for friends. These LRGs might have been a one-off event, or an event happened for a couple of years in a row, but were never recorded, leaving those games to have been lost to history. Most of these early LRG creators likely had no idea that there were other fans out there creating similar games.

There is one exception. *Survivor Angelica* is likely the oldest and continually running annual *Survivor*-style LRG. This game was originally created by a group of friends in 2002 who all shared a common passion for *Survivor*. While the game was known as *Survivor Weekend* initially, it evolved over time and grew in scope, now casting players from all over the country as well as filming and posting seasons onto *YouTube*. We know of a few other earlier games thanks to YouTube. For example, *Survivor Backyard* was a game run by Jake Spartz from 2006 to 2015 in his family's backyard. Each season consisted of 8 to 18 players and posted episodes on *YouTube* for friends and fans to watch.

YouTube has played a pivotal role in forming and developing the LRG community. Two notable games that took the time to film, edit, and post episodes onto *YouTube* are *Survivor British Columbia* and *Surviving Reelfoot. Survivor British Columbia* was founded by Jireh Batulan in 2012. His fourth season, "The Battle of BC," currently has 14.000 views on *YouTube. Surviving Reelfoot* has likely had the most success of any game with airing its seasons on *YouTube*. Founded in 2012 by Amos Smith, the game's second season, "Orange County," currently has 40,000 views on *YouTube* for its premiere episode!

The success of these seasons and others in the mid-2010s on

YouTube had several beneficial outcomes on the greater LRG community. First, it drew attention to fans that games like these, experiences akin to a TV show they loved, existed. This then gave rise to social media pages on *Facebook* or *Instagram* dedicated to LRGs. Social media not only connected fans together, who could then apply to these games, but also connected LRG hosts who never knew that there were other like them out there. Finally, these games airing on *YouTube* inspired others to create and host their own LRGs.

The number of LRGs in existence continue to grow and expand. As new reality TV shows air, such as *The Traitors*, new games are launched based off those shows. More LRGs are being formed with original formats, where games may just take inspiration from preexisting reality TV shows instead of mimicking those formats. Through both the increase in the number of games founded, as well as the continued discovery of games that have been operating and the greater community just didn't know about them, there are now around 300 games of various styles, length, and formats in existence as of 2026 that we know of.

It's hard to predict where the future will take LRGs. Hopefully though, the future is promising and both the creation of new games as well as player demand for games will continue to grow.

Part One

Belonging Begins with Courage

Belonging does not begin when everyone welcomes you. It begins when you decide to step forward anyway. Before creation, before building, before game day, before alliances, before confessionals, and before someone says your name with trust, there is the quiet act of arrival. The stories that follow are about that first courageous choice — to enter the room, to risk being seen, to believe there might be a place for you here. Every game starts with a step. Every belonging starts with someone willing to take it.

"You can be completely out of your element—and still be exactly where you belong."

~Alicia Garza

ALICIA GARZA

LIVESTREAM HOST

2025

"I always thought I would be one of these people that only did one thing... and then I grew up, and then I grew up again."

Alicia didn't whisper it.

"Record away," she laughed. "I'm about to live my life online."

She said it like a logistics note, not a confession. Not the kind of sentence people usually soften or defend. I could hear the tiny adjustments of someone settling into a call, the brush of fabric against a microphone, a breath drawn in and released slowly, the ease of someone who has stopped asking permission to be fully visible.

"I quit my job a year ago," she added. "And I have not gone back."

Some people ease into reinvention quietly. Not Alicia. She calls it what it is without hesitation. She was done pretending that one career, one version of success, or one inherited blueprint was ever going to contain her.

She learned early that if she wanted to be held, she might have to build the circle herself.

Alicia's upbringing wasn't gentle. She talks openly about distance from family, about learning young that proximity does not guarantee safety. Friendship, for her, wasn't decorative. It was structural. It was how you survived loneliness without collapsing into it.

"I know where it comes from," she said simply. "It comes from not being close to my family and having a really difficult growing up situation and really needing to rely on friends and have friends to be that love in my life."

As she spoke, I found myself circling a question I didn't yet know would guide this entire book:

What do we build when the life we inherited doesn't feel like home?

There are people who inherit belonging and there are people who must construct it. Alicia belongs to the latter.

"My favorite thing about myself," she told me, "is that I'm a really great friend."

She says it proudly.

Six best friends. Chosen deliberately. Built with loyalty, with presence, and with the kind of reliability that shows up when everything else falls apart. When she talks about them, you can feel the architecture of it... how love can be constructed intentionally, beam by beam.

The instinct to build belonging instead of waiting for it runs through everything Alicia touches. Her *Survivor* story didn't begin in the woods. It began in a college apartment in 2012.

She was a super senior, stuck on the last class she needed to graduate. Her closest friends had moved on. The apartment she lived in felt hollow... hallway silence, doors closing softly but decisively, the hum of a refrigerator louder than it should be, the faint smell of stale coffee clinging to the air. She remembers lying on her bed staring at the thin crack in the ceiling above her, tracing it with her eyes like it might open and lead somewhere better.

The dishes in the sink weren't hers and the conversations in the kitchen weren't meant for her.

It is a specific kind of loneliness—being surrounded by noise and still feeling erased by solitude.

When she found an online *Survivor*-format game buried in a *Reddit* thread, she applied. She played. And it was then that something in her spine straightened.

It wasn't strategy that hooked her.

It was recognition.

Being liked. Being chosen. Being included in late-night chats that stretched past midnight, her laptop balanced on her knees, the fan humming warm against her skin. The glow of the screen lighting her face in an otherwise dark room.

On Alicia's first *Skype* call, voices overlapped, laughter arrived half a second delayed but still landing, her heart beating faster as if she had stepped into a real room instead of a digital one.

It felt like a door opening.

Not just to a game, but to a different kind of belonging.

"It was a rare moment in my life where my confidence was low," she said. "And realizing that people really liked me for me—that was very impactful at that time."

As she described it, I realized she hadn't simply found a distraction. She had found raw material. A different blueprint. A space where she didn't have to audition for acceptance.

ORGs led to friendships. Friendships led to travel. Travel led to a life shaped less by geography and more by people. Alicia road-tripped across the country in a giant loop, dust gathering on the dashboard, playlists running out and starting again, pulling into driveways she'd only seen in profile pictures. Hugging people she had known through screens. Sitting at kitchen tables where she didn't have to explain why this community mattered.

The bridge metaphor wasn't conceptual. It was literal. And then something else shifted...

Alicia grew up in a conservative Texas household. Certain assumptions were ambient. Certain boundaries unquestioned. There was a time she didn't believe a woman should be president. A time she didn't believe gay marriage should exist.

Then she met *Survivor* people.

Queer people. Open people. Generous people.

They didn't debate her into transformation. They invited her into rooms. They cooked dinner. They laughed loudly, shoulder to shoulder, music playing from someone's phone speaker on the counter. People being people and living fully.

"They were the best people I'd ever met," she said. "Inclusive. Friendly. Fun."

And slowly, almost imperceptibly at first, the edges of her worldview softened. You can't unsee humanity once you've been welcomed by it.

◆

Alicia has never played in a LRG. The woods intimidate her. She's scared of the dark. Spiders are her worst fear. She jokes that if she ever showed up as a player, people would stare in disbelief. I can picture it: her stepping carefully over uneven ground, the rustle of leaves making her shoulders lift instinctively.

And yet, she found her footing in the woods when Alicia became a livestream host.

The voice that carries the game to the people who cannot physically be there. The parents watching from living rooms. The partners refreshing links. The friends texting commentary in group chats.

She translates chaos into narrative.

The first time she slipped on a headset, she felt its weight press gently against her temples. The sun was sharp that day. The air smelled like damp earth and sawdust. Cameras whirred. A challenge reset mid-stream. Someone shouted off-frame. She felt the adrenaline spike in her chest... and kept talking. Kept translating. Kept steadying the experience for everyone watching from home.

When cameras shake. When audio drops. When players scatter and something pivotal happens just out of frame, Alicia becomes the thread the audience can hold.

She didn't plan for that role.

She missed the meeting where responsibilities were divided. Later, she checked the list and saw it next to her name: Livestream Queen.

"I am there for the loved ones," she said. "I'm not there for the players. Everyone's family and loved ones will know who I am. And the players are like, who are you? And it's not until the next year when they come back that they're like, oh my God—my mother's obsessed with you."

She had never watched a livestream. Never hosted one. So she studied. She watched other streams. Took notes. Learned pacing. Found her tone—warm, quick, emotionally attuned without becoming spectacle. And slowly, the headset stopped feeling foreign. The camera stopped feeling intimidating.

That first full season she discovered something she hadn't expected.

"I've never been more out of my element, but also in my element at the same time," she said. "I was just surrounded by fellow Survivor lover-players that were so passionate—not only about *Survivor*, but about each other and about everything."

She realized something quietly powerful: you can be completely out of your element and still be exactly where you belong.

The lesson that changed her most didn't come from success.

It came from exhaustion.

Early seasons, she carried everything because she could. Pre-game planning. Player check-in. Stream management. Crisis smoothing. She pushed until halfway through each game when the pressure crested and spilled over, her jaw tight, voice sharper than she meant it to be, heat rising behind her eyes while she smiled through it on camera. The kind of tired that hums in your bones. The kind where even when you mute your microphone, your shoulders stay lifted and braced as if something might collapse without you holding it.

Season seven was different.

Fewer volunteers. More pressure.

Allen and Kadie (Yannone) saw what Alicia couldn't. They didn't critique her. They protected her instead.

Kadie made Alicia take ten-minute breaks. Real ones. Step outside. Drink water. Let her headset rest on the table. As she stood alone in the quiet, away from cameras and chatter, she felt the sun on her face without needing to narrate it. She let her shoulders drop and felt the air move in and out of her lungs without urgency.

"I am not a robot," she said. "I am a human being. I need to rest."

I realized something as she said it... the question wasn't just what do we build when the life we inherited doesn't feel like home?

It was also: *Can we build in such a way that doesn't consume us?*

◆

When she talks about game access now, about sponsorships, stipends, lowering barriers... I hear someone who remembers what it felt like to stand outside a door.

"It would be nice that the volunteers that come one day didn't have to pay for the Airbnb," she said. "It would be nice if players can't make the entry fee, that's not a big deal. Come along anyway. We just want you here."

Her vision isn't about scale. It's about welcome. And maybe that is her answer.

She built rooms. And then she learned to leave space inside them for herself.

MY LENS REFRAMED

Alicia redefined reinvention for me.

It is not instability... it is alignment. It is the moment you stop performing "fine" and begin building something that actually fits.

Her way of moving through the world brings a kind of clarity that stays with you. It draws your attention to the spaces we remain in simply because they are familiar... even when they no longer hold us. There is courage in the way she chooses differently... without needing everything to be certain first.

Reinvention, as I have come to understand it here, is not a reaction... it is a decision. A willingness to choose truth over comfort... even when the path forward has not fully taken shape.

What do we build when the life we inherited does not feel like home?

If Alicia is any indication... we build with care. We create spaces where people can exhale... where belonging is not something that has to be earned... where people are welcomed as they are.

A life that fits is rarely found.

It is created... moment by moment... choice by choice.

And sometimes, the most powerful thing you can do... is build the space you once needed.

Carlos Kiddo
Player • ORG Creator

2024

"I had to look at myself in the mirror and realize that there were a lot of things in my real life that I covered up."

There are players who love the win, and players who love the fight. Carlos loves the moment right before both... the moment when your body tells you to shrink, but your mind decides to stay.

He is reflective in a way that feels rare. Simply honest. You hear it in how he pauses before answering, like he's reaching for the truest version of a moment instead of the cleanest. You hear it in how he revisits scenes without rushing to justify them. Like someone who learned early that safety isn't a personality trait, it's something you build.

Carlos is twenty-six, living in Lubbock, Texas, earning his PhD in clinical psychology. The detail matters, not because it sounds impressive (it is), but because it explains something you feel before you can name it: Carlos doesn't just play these games. He studies them... human behavior under pressure, the shape of trust, the quiet math of fear moving through a group before anyone admits it's there.

He lives with intention around boundaries. At one point, he even created an alias, not to hide, but to protect. To keep worlds from collapsing into each other.

Not secrecy.

Safety.

Carlos didn't begin in the woods.

He began online.

A *Survivor* fan tweeting into the void, he was found by someone who asked if he wanted to play one of "these games." His answer was immediate. "I was like, what are those?" he told me. "So I applied, I played and then won."

That first win planted a dangerous idea: I could win all of them.

He smiles at that now—the way you smile at your younger self: brilliant, bold, and incomplete... but full of courage, adventure, and belief.

From *Twitter*, he moved to *Skype*. Text-only games started to feel thin. *Skype* added what mattered most... presence, tone, and timing. The micro-moments where alliances are born and broken. The half-second hesitations that tell you someone is lying. The warmth of a laugh that means connection or camouflage, depending on who's holding it.

Then he hosted.

Then repetition dulled the edge.

So he changed the conditions.

Alias-based games. New identities. No reputational shortcuts. Every season demanded adaptation. No coasting. No familiarity to lean on.

Eventually, the final step called him.

In-person.

Carlos has played five live reality games.

He hasn't won. His highest placement is fifth.

He doesn't say this apologetically. He says it like someone who understands data: outcomes matter, but patterns matter more. What Carlos tracks isn't placement.

It's pressure... pressure reveals things winning never does.

When asked which experiences felt most legitimate, Carlos pointed first to *Surviving Reelfoot,* then to *Surviving Bloomington*—high praise from someone fluent across formats. He spoke about Bloomington's intentional design: allowing small comfort items. A toothbrush. A mat. A snack.

Things that sound minor until you understand what deprivation does to the nervous system.

"Small things make a difference," he said. Being able to brush his teeth each morning and evening changed something. Not the experience —the experience was still hard—but the quality of how the hardship landed. "It didn't feel like this dirtiness," he said, searching for the right words. "It was still rough. I personally didn't bring snacks, so I was still hungry."

Brushing your teeth doesn't make you spoiled. It makes you human. You're still outside. Still hungry. Still wet. Still calculating every look, every pause, every shift in energy.

Comfort doesn't erase hardship. It changes how hardship feels.

◆

Carlos lights up when he talks about hosting. Playing gives him intensity. Hosting gives him clarity.

He loves the analysis. The architecture of strategy. The social mechanics, without the personal risk of collapse. Graduate school limits his time, so he hosts minis: compressed, high-intensity games that deliver everything he loves in a tighter frame.

Sometimes he plans weeks ahead. Sometimes the decision is made in a moment. "If I finish my homework or if I finish this thing," he told me, "I'm going to reward myself by hosting a mini tonight." The impulse is genuine—not procrastination, but permission. A way of saying: I need this, and I know how to build it.

Hosting isn't escape. It's regulation.

◆

Carlos is deeply self-aware. Still, his first in-person game exposed something he hadn't yet faced.

He arrived late.

Everyone else was already there talking, connecting, forming early impressions. His body reacted before his mind could intervene. Anxiety surged, not the manageable kind you can mask briefly, but the full-body kind.

He described it like walking into a freezer. "Literally from head to toe, I felt just completely shook. I froze," he said. "I did not really initiate talking to other people. I was very internalized."

That image landed because you can feel it: the sudden cold, the lock-up, the way your breath turns shallow. The way your limbs stop feeling like allies and start feeling like evidence.

He stopped initiating conversation. Turned inward. Assumed he was finished before he began. And this time, there was no screen to close and no place to hide.

People could see his legs shaking. See him go quiet. See him trying to disappear.

Later, he realized something unsettling: real life had allowed him to manage certain wounds by never staying uncomfortable long enough for them to split open.

The game held him there.

These games don't create fear.

They reveal it.

◆

Carlos understands how absurd this might sound to people who have never played.

No prize. No paycheck. People spend money on flights, hotels, bruises, and heartbreak.

Why?

People train for marathons. People pay for mud runs. People invest deeply in things that leave them exhausted and changed. We don't call that foolish.

We call it passion.

LRGs, Carlos says, are a space where you spend money on something that genuinely engages you. The value isn't the title.

The value is presence.

The value is discovering who you are when it's hard.

One of Carlos' most vivid memories came from *Surviving Reelfoot*.

Bottom of the tribe. Barely surviving. Then rain. Cold. Wet clothes. No sleep. A burn from standing too close to the fire trying to dry his clothes. Pain layered onto exhaustion... the kind that makes your thoughts feel heavy and your patience feel thin.

"Is this worth it? I am shivering," he told himself that night. "My whole body was very cold throughout the night. My clothes were wet." He was at the bottom of his tribe, certain he was going home next. The burn on his arm. The cold that would not break. And underneath it all, that one honest question: is this worth it?

Then, without warning, a twist. A swap. A second life handed to him mid-collapse.

The relief was immediate and almost unbelievable. "It's like I have a new life," he said. And then, just as quickly, the new tribe put him back at the bottom. The graph went low, then high, then low again—all within hours. And then another twist. Another rock. Another store. Another chance. "You can't even explain it as much as I'm trying to explain it," he said. "Imagine living through it."

Believing you're finished, then being asked to stand up and play again.

Burned.

Freezing.

Almost gone.

He asked the only question that mattered: Is this worth it? His answer wasn't bravado. It was continuity. He stayed.

◆

When the conversation turned to inclusion and safety, Carlos didn't moralize.

He diagnosed. He identified the fear many people live inside—the fear of saying the wrong thing, of engaging imperfectly, of exposure. "There is a lot of fear in engaging in conversations," he said. "A lot of people could grow and a lot of people could learn and move forward from those conversations—but fear holds them back. And what that fear produces is not neutrality. It produces avoidance that still causes harm, just quietly, from a distance. You see these things coming up in ways that a lot of people are unintentional about," he continued, "and they still come up and they're still hurtful."

Avoidance doesn't protect anyone.

It delays growth.

Ultimately, Carlos believes this community can evolve—but only if inclusivity is intentional. In casting. In structure. In how people are treated during the game, not just before it.

Safety does not happen by accident.

My Lens Reframed

This is not a chapter about winning. It is about something far more human. It is about what it looks like to enter a room knowing your body may freeze... and choosing to stay anyway.

There is a kind of courage in that choice that reshaped how I understand perseverance. It is not built in comfort. It is formed in the moments where leaving would be easier... and something in you decides to step in and step up. To stay inside yourself... even when everything in your body is asking you to walk away.

Carlos reveals something deeper than outcome. He shows what it means to be present in real time... without certainty, without protection, without the promise that the moment will resolve cleanly. Courage, here, is not what I thought it was. It is not dominance. It is not control. It is not the absence of fear.

It is the decision to stay... while it is still there.

And in that choice, something else becomes visible. What these spaces are really asking of us is not only strategy... not only performance... but something underneath all of it. The unguarded, human self that surfaces when the pressure is real... the part of us that cannot hide once the moment asks more than we planned to give.

Some players chase the crown.

Carlos draws attention somewhere deeper... to the truth we are willing to face about ourselves in those moments.

Sometimes the most valuable thing we bring home is not a title...

Brittany J.

Player

2024

"If I fail, I fail."

Brittany does not simply enter a space... she warms it. There is an ease to her presence that settles gently over a room, something light and unforced that invites people to soften without realizing why. Her laughter arrives easily. Her eyes meet yours fully. There is openness in the way she carries herself, a kind of quiet welcome that shifts the atmosphere around her. Conversations begin to flow more naturally. Shoulders lower. People exhale. It would be easy to stop there, to describe her as sunshine and let that be enough.

But then you watch her play.

Something deeper begins to reveal itself. The warmth is real, unmistakably so, but it is not the whole story. Beneath it lives something steady and grounded. Not sharp, not hardened, not showy in any way... just enduring. A quiet strength that does not need to announce itself because it has already been tested. It is the kind of grit that has moved through difficulty without needing to retell it for validation. It simply exists, woven into who she is.

Brittany is thirty-two and from Bloomington, Indiana. She is a wife and a mother of two, one still small enough to reach for her hand and one already stretching toward independence. There is an eleven-year-old dog folded into the rhythm of their home, completing a picture that feels both full and deeply familiar. Her days are shaped by the ordinary details that hold a family together... snack schedules, bedtime routines, school forms tucked into backpacks. There is nothing flashy about it, and yet there is something profoundly meaningful in the steadiness of that life. It is the kind of fullness that asks for everything and gives everything back in return, one quiet moment at a time.

Still... she chose to step into the woods.

"I love doing things out of my comfort zone," she says. "I like to push myself. There's something about when you do it, it makes you feel so proud."

That is the through line. She is not drawn to these experiences because they are easy or flattering. She is drawn to them because they are not. Because they ask something real of her. Because they create space for a version of herself that does not emerge in comfort.

Some people chase recognition. Some chase the outcome. Brittany moves toward the version of herself that only appears when something is difficult. She understands that pain is part of that process, but she also understands that it does not last forever.

◆

Brittany's story does not begin with *Survivor*. It begins with movement.

She was a swimmer first, shaped by the discipline of repetition and the solitude of water. There is something formative about that environment, about learning to push forward stroke after stroke with only the rhythm of your own breath to guide you. The smell of chlorine lingering in her hair, the echo of whistles against tile, the quiet determination it takes to return to the water again and again... these were the early foundations of her strength. In high school, she added cross country, not because she loved running, but because she understood what it could give her. It was another way to build endurance, another way to expand what her body and mind could hold.

After graduation, she did not stop.

Movement had already become a language she spoke fluently.

Triathlons came next, and she approached them with the same commitment that had shaped her from the beginning. For eight years, she trained, raced, and refined her understanding of what it meant to endure. Early mornings became routine. Long rides stretched her limits. Breath and effort began to move in sync, each reinforcing the other. She was not dabbling. She was building something within herself, layer by layer.

"My dad can't believe how strong I am at everything," she told me. "He's like, you just put your hundred percent into everything you're going to do at that moment."

She had no argument with that. It is simply how she is made.

Somewhere along the way, *Survivor* entered her world through conversation. It was not a singular moment of revelation, but something that grew over time. She and a coworker would talk through episodes, dissect strategy, revisit decisions, and carry the story with them into the next day. It became something they turned over and examined, not just as entertainment, but as something worth understanding.

She had a player she measured herself against. A standard she quietly held.

"Sarah Lacina," she said simply. "She's got little kids. She runs marathons all over the place. She's amazing. We both have grit and passion."

That identification was not accidental. It told me something about how Brittany sees herself—not as someone who watches from the outside, but as someone who belongs in the game.

Then, in 2019, the idea became real.

She heard that someone from her high school was hosting a live *Survivor*—style game in Martinsville, Indiana (*Survivor Indiana*). Twelve hours of competition, strategy, and social pressure, all unfolding in real time. She did not romanticize the opportunity. She evaluated it with a kind of grounded honesty that feels distinctly her own.

"I had the strength, the stamina to do the challenges," she told me, "and I think I'm social enough. I just wanted to see how far I could go."

There is something powerful in that kind of self-awareness, in the ability to step forward without exaggeration and without fear of being wrong.

She played.

She made the merge. She placed seventh. She found a hidden immunity idol and used it to save herself at a critical moment. She did not win the game, but she left with something that stayed with her long after it ended. She left with proof. Proof of what she could do, what she could withstand, and who she could be when placed in something unfamiliar.

Her relationship with difficulty is not theoretical.

In 2015, she was training for her first full Ironman. Six days before a 70.3*, a major milestone she had worked toward for months, she went out for a ride. A car hit her.

At first, she stood. There is something instinctive in that response, a desire to believe you are still okay, still capable of continuing. Then her body responded with a truth she could not ignore. When she tried to move, her femur broke. The sound, the shift, the undeniable reality of it... those moments imprint themselves in a way that does not fade.

The hospital held both physical pain and something quieter but equally profound. There is a particular kind of grief that comes from watching a goal dissolve after months of discipline. It is not just the loss of the event, but the loss of everything that led up to it.

Then the story shifted again.

After surgery, while she was learning how to move through even the simplest tasks, an MRI revealed that a blood clot had traveled to her lung. It was close. Close enough that survival itself entered the

---

* A 70.3 or "Half-Ironman," is a long-distance triathlon consisting of a 1.2-mile (1.9 km) swim, 56-mile (90 km) bike ride, and 13.1-mile (21.1 km) run.

conversation in a way it had not before. They removed it. They saved her life.

Recovery did not feel triumphant from the inside. It was slow. It was humbling. It looked like five minutes on a treadmill at the lowest possible pace, her breath uneven, her body unfamiliar to her. The environment was sterile, filled with the quiet hum of machines. Her resting heart rate no longer reflected the athlete she had been. It was a beginning again, whether she had chosen it or not.

Brittany describes that early recovery with a kind of stark clarity: "I was able to walk for five minutes at 1.0 pace on the treadmill and I was out of breath five minutes in, and I was like, I'm never going to be able to run again. This is not going to be good." But she also reveals something about how she moves through that despair. "I just have an overdrive and I just am like the pain is temporary. You just push yourself and I'm always going to give it my all."

So she began.

By July, she ran again. It was only half a mile, and it was not perfect, but it was real. It was movement forward.

By August, she stood at the beginning of another moment. She got married, and she walked down the aisle without crutches. There is something quietly profound about that image, about choosing to walk forward while everything in your life bears witness to what you have moved through.

She did not let the interruption redefine the dream.

In 2016, she returned to it.

She completed the *Ironman*. Her husband trained alongside her every step of the way—weekend rides stretching to a hundred and twenty miles, the rain ride across Indiana in July, weeks of shared early mornings. Then, at the finish, he stepped back. He allowed that moment to belong fully to her.

"I came across that finish line and it was the most magical moment ever," she said.

The numbers tell part of the story: she ran a 3:52 marathon after biking 115 miles, finishing fifth in her age group. "I don't know where that came from," she said, "but I just have an overdrive."

She crossed that line carrying not just endurance, but the lived understanding that being knocked down had not defined her. It is a kind of partnership that understands both presence and space, knowing when to walk beside and when to release.

When Brittany speaks about choosing the hard thing, she is speaking from experience.

◆

And yet, her greatest challenge does not live in her physical endurance.

It lives in her heart.

The most difficult part of these games for her is not the cold or the hunger or even the pressure. It is the moment when someone has to go home. She does not take pleasure in causing harm. She does not view betrayal as entertainment. She understands the structure of the game and can hold that truth, but she also understands that people carry these experiences with them long after they end.

"I just don't want to hurt anybody," she says simply. "That's the total downfall."

The essence of that statement speaks to Brittany's heart. She has watched people leave these games carrying more than just disappointment. She understands the emotional architecture of what happens when you are voted out by people you have come to trust.

"People do leave hurt," she says, her voice steady. "And it could be for a week. For some people it's a month. For some people it's a year."

There is an awareness here that extends beyond game mechanics. She recognizes that what happens in the woods does not stay in the woods. It travels home. It settles into people. It becomes part of their story.

But what makes Brittany distinct is not simply that she feels this tension. It is that she acts on it, even when doing so works against her own strategic interests.

◆

I remember the moment clearly. We were deep enough into the

game that alliances had solidified and targets had begun to form. I shared with her that I knew I was vulnerable. That people were circling. That I could feel the shift in conversations, the way certain players had begun to avoid my eyes.

Brittany listened without interruption. She did not dismiss my concern or offer false reassurance. She simply took it in, the way she takes in most things... fully and without performance.

Then, quietly, she gave me an advantage.

She did not make a show of it. She did not ask for anything in return. She did not position it as a move that would bind me to her or create leverage she could use later. She simply recognized that I was in danger, and she had something that could help, and so she gave it. The decision was clean. It was immediate. It reflected something foundational about how she moves through these spaces.

She understood what that advantage meant. She knew its value within the structure of the game. She knew that holding onto it could protect her own position or create opportunities down the line. And still, she chose to use it in service of someone else's safety. Not because it advanced her strategically, but because it aligned with something deeper... with the part of her that cannot watch someone struggle without offering what she has to give.

That moment stays with me because it was so entirely her. It was Brittany holding both truths at once. She was playing the game with full awareness of its mechanics, and she was also refusing to let those mechanics strip away her instinct to protect. She did not see those things as contradictory. She simply moved through the tension between them with a kind of grace that most people never find.

Her tenderness intact.

◆

Brittany left her games not with a sense of mastery, but with awareness.

She recognized that people trust her. They seek her out. They confide in her. When the energy in a group shifts, she is someone others naturally turn toward. She learned that she can lead, that she can communicate clearly, that she can steady a space when others begin to lose their footing.

"I learned how strong I was on things that I would've never tried," she reflects. "Some challenges I didn't think I'd be good at, and shockingly I was pretty okay at."

What others did not always see was how much was running beneath the surface.

"I was talking to people after and they were like, oh, I didn't realize you were thinking all these thoughts," she said. "My brain never stops. I'm always thinking about who's working with who and where."

That is the paradox she carries into every game. The warmth disarms. The strategy moves quietly beneath it. She is playing—make no mistake—and she is doing so with full attention and intention.

But she also recognized something more subtle and more important. Her energy, her enthusiasm, her engagement with the moment can sometimes move faster than the people around her. It does not come from ego, but from aliveness, from being fully present. Still, she understands the importance of pacing, of allowing others to find their place within the rhythm of the group.

"Sometimes I get a little bit too hyped up about events," she acknowledges without defensiveness, "and I need to calm down, take a back seat, listen to others, and let them take control. I can be overbearing, and I got to take a backseat."

That kind of awareness is not given lightly. It is learned through experience and reflection, through being willing to see yourself not just in your strengths, but in your patterns. Brittany moves through this recognition without shame or self-criticism. She is simply naming what she has learned about herself and committing to the refinement that comes with knowing better.

◆

Motherhood, for Brittany, is not simply a role she holds. It is something she inhabits fully. And still, she named something that many women experience quietly over time. When you live within that role long enough, the world begins to see you through that single lens.

You become the one who manages, organizes, supports, and sustains. It is meaningful work, but it can also narrow the way others perceive you.

"Whenever you're in the motherly role, you get lost in that," Brittany reflects. "It becomes your full identity."

The weight of that observation settles in. There is no bitterness in her voice—only clarity. She loves her children with the kind of fierceness that shapes days and seasons. And yet, something quieter has also been true. There has been a dimming, not of her care or commitment, but of the other facets of who she is. The athlete. The risk-taker. The woman who pushes toward difficult things.

When Brittany stepped into *Surviving Bloomington*, something shifted.

People saw her.

Not as a role or a function, but as herself. A fellow player told her how personable and friendly she was—and that she had never once brought up her kids during the whole game.

"For her saying that," Brittany said, her voice dropping just slightly, "it made me feel really good. I don't want to cry because that's me inside. To step out and be your true self and have people like you for being yourself, it makes you feel really good as a mom," she says. "Because you're still in there. You're more than just your kids or your family. You are still a really passionate and driven person deep down inside."

She pauses, then adds a newly earned recognition, "It feels really good to push yourself and just be you again and know that you're still there... that you didn't disappear."

She had never disappeared. She had simply not been witnessed.

Being seen again in your fullness in an empowering experience we should all experience... but many never do.

These experiences, for all of their intensity, create space for that kind of recognition. They remove the familiar structures long enough to remind you that you are not limited to the roles you carry. You are more layered than that, more expansive, more whole.

◆

Brittany returned home changed in ways that were both subtle and significant.

"It's going to make you a better mom when you come back," she said, thinking now of the women who might be reading, "to know that you can do something that tough. It's going to make you a better mom, wife, everything. Whenever you get home, you're going to feel so much stronger, and it's going to build that bond with your family even more."

She became more present. More attentive. Less pulled toward distraction and more anchored in the moments that make up her daily life. The rhythm of her home shifted as well. Her children leaned into their father in new ways, not because she stepped away, but because she allowed space to be shared.

"I had learned how to communicate with so many different people out there," she said, "different communication styles and what worked for people. And so now we communicate better too. It brought it all together."

She did not become more by doing more.

She became more by remembering that she exists beyond what she gives.

My Lens Reframed

What stays with me, as I sit with Brittany's story, is not simply her brightness or her endurance, but the way she holds both without conflict. Her warmth is not separate from her strength, and her strength does not diminish her softness. They exist together, naturally, creating a presence that feels both inviting and grounded. It reminds me that we are not required to choose between being gentle and being strong. We are allowed to be both.

Her life offers a definition of strength that extends beyond the moments of visible endurance. It is present in her willingness to continue choosing what is difficult without allowing that difficulty to harden her. That kind of courage settles into character. It shapes the way she moves through the world and leaves a lasting impression on those who encounter her.

And it deepens something in me as I reflect on it... a gentler understanding of strength. One that does not ask us to dim our light or disappear inside the roles we hold for others. One that allows us to stay connected to ourselves, even as we show up fully for the people we love.

Brittany did not enter these spaces to prove that she was unbreakable.

She entered... and in doing so, found her way back to a part of herself that had always been there.

Zach Fifer
Player • Creator

2024

"Every time I leave a game, I understand myself a little more."

What does it mean to hold onto a moment... and how do you prove to yourself that it was real?

Zach does not collect things in the way most people do. He collects evidence. Not of status or achievement, but of presence. Of having lived inside something fully enough that it left a mark. When he tells me about his move to San Diego, he does not begin with the ocean or the promise of what is next. He begins with the boxes. Half opened, half sorted, scattered across hardwood floors in a space that has not yet decided what it will become.

Inside those boxes are not expensive items or carefully curated displays. They are small, sentimental pieces of a life that refuse to be forgotten. Letters. Notes. Cards with handwriting that carries memory in a way no photograph ever could.

He laughs when he calls them *tchotchkes*, as if to soften the truth of it. The word lands lightly, but what it holds is anything but. Each object is a tether. A way to reach back and touch a version of himself that existed in a specific place, at a specific time, with specific people. He tells me that sometimes he will open an old card and suddenly understand why he kept it. A single line in his mother's handwriting— *I'm proud of you* —and the room shifts. The past becomes present. The feeling returns without asking permission.

That is not clutter.

It is an inanimate witness.

A beautiful confirmation.

Before we ever talk about games, I understand something essential about Zach. He is not trying to hold onto the past because he is afraid of moving forward. He is trying to carry it with him, intact, so that nothing meaningful is lost in the transition. He has learned, in ways that feel both gentle and hard won, that tenderness can slip away if it is not held with intention.

His story, like so many in this community, begins with *Survivor*. Even here, there is a shift that feels distinctly his. During the pandemic, when the world paused and *Survivor* disappeared from its usual rhythm, Zach felt the absence in a way that surprised him. It was not just entertainment that was missing. It was ritual. It was structure. It was a space where something inside him had learned to come alive. He said it plainly, and the line has stayed with me because it reveals so much about the way he moves through the world. "I want *Survivor* for myself... and I don't know what to do."

Some people would have waited.

Zach built.

He gathered friends, asked them to quarantine within their own circles, and created a multi-day *Survivor*-experience as a birthday celebration. Not something casual or symbolic, but something immersive. Something that asked people to show up fully. There were challenges. There were torches. There were stakes that did not need to be manufactured because the moment people commit, the stakes become real on their own.

That experience did not end when the game ended.

It revealed something.

When the door he had been waiting for did not open, he did not stand outside it.

He built a new one.

♦

When I ask him what it says about him that his instinct was to build a game before he even knew this community existed, he does not pause. He traces the answer back with care.

"My mom is such an incredible host," he said. "Growing up, if I had friends coming over—regardless of whether they say yes or no, she's like, here's chips and salsa, here's some snacky nuts. She's so good at making people feel welcome." He smiled. "And then my dad on the other side is such a creative person—instead of just going to the movie theater, he would make a scavenger hunt for us. It's very *Survivor*-coded."

Hospitality and imagination lived side by side in his childhood, shaping a way of seeing the world that would later become foundational to how he creates. Then theater entered his life, adding another layer. Story, character, immersion.

Zach does not experience these games as isolated events. He understands them as living narratives, spaces where people reveal who they are under pressure and where growth is not a byproduct, but the point.

He wants to win. That truth is present. When Zach plays, he does not just participate. He maps. He plays with intention and focus. Still, the core of what drives him lives somewhere else.

"I'm here to have fun, make connections, and create memories," Zach's smile, now wide and full. "If I win, if I lose, as long as I can walk away and be proud of myself and have these new connections—*that's what I'm in it for.*"

♦

That perspective deepens when he talks about the difference

between one-day games and those that stretch overnight. Time changes everything. When you sleep near people, when hunger carries into morning, when the night creates space for conversations that would never happen in daylight, something shifts.

"Laying there at one in the morning and you can't sleep," Zach said, "and it's connecting with people and it's like talking about family and home and what you're hungry for—that is the game right there. And I don't think you can really capture that on camera."

The game loosens its grip as the human experience deepens. Trust forms differently. Laughter lands softer. The relationships that emerge feel less like strategy and more like something that might last.

That is the version of the game that stays with him.

That is the version he carries forward.

♦

Zach is honest about the parts of himself that are still evolving. He speaks about a version of himself shaped by perfection, by achievement, by a quiet belief that if he did things well enough, the outcome would follow. That belief held until it did not.

"I remember losing and having this wave of emotions crash over me," he said of his first game. "I did not expect it to hurt this much." He paused before continuing. "Walking away from that made me remember that putting all your eggs in one basket—not saying that you shouldn't fight and really reach for what you want—but life isn't always going to be how you want it to be. And that's fine."

The lesson was not about strategy.

It was about life.

You can prepare and still be surprised. You can care deeply and still lose. You can show up fully and still find yourself on the outside of something you wanted to be inside.

Regret does not carry you forward. Learning does.

♦

Zach lost a close friend during his senior year of high school. In her farewell notes, she left him something he has never set down.

"Find happiness, because happiness is the one true gift in life."

He said quietly. "I live by that mantra every single day—*how can I be happier now? How can I work toward a life that's filled with as much happiness as possible?* To obtain that, you have to go through some tough challenges."

That mantra does not make the hard things easier. It makes them meaningful. It gives him a framework for moving through difficulty without losing the thread of who he is or where he is going.

"Bravery isn't the absence of fear," he said. "It's fear itself... it is getting hit and getting back up. It is being fearful and being able to face that fear."

♦

Zach's voice shifts when he we talk about his hosting journey. There is a weight there that feels different from the rest of the conversation. He has seen what happens when games cross a line, when intensity moves beyond challenge and into harm. He has sat with the question that every thoughtful creator eventually faces. What am I building, and what does it cost the people inside it?

His answer was not to step away. It was to build better.

Structure became the answer. Not as restriction, but as protection. Physical safety, yes, but also emotional and relational safety. Names. Pronouns. Boundaries. Consent. A container strong enough to hold intensity without allowing it to fracture the people inside it. When he talks about what these spaces can become, he does not sound theoretical. He sounds protective. He sounds responsible. He sounds like someone who understands that care is not separate from play. It is what makes meaningful play possible in the first place.

Safety is not softness. It is structure.

♦

Zach does not offer a neatly defined future. He offers something more honest. A posture. A willingness to move toward what feels true, even when it carries uncertainty. He speaks about the people who have shaped him—his family, his partner, the friends from games who became something more permanent—with a tenderness that suggests he understands exactly what he is building toward.

"Given the opportunity, that would be the dream," he said when the conversation turned to what comes next. "I have this pipe dream of getting a property—Michigan or upstate New York—kind of like an adult summer camp. Its main purpose would be to do these games. And the lessons you learn speak for themselves."

He is building a life that holds both foundation and possibility. Work, home, future family—all of it taking shape alongside a continued commitment to play.

That tension is not something he is trying to resolve.

It is something he is learning to live inside.

MY LENS REFRAMED

Zach led me to reconsider the way I think about *memory*. I have often thought of it as something that fades unless it is held tightly. What I see in him offers a different way of carrying it... one that is more intentional, more attentive, and far more lasting.

Memory does not have to be forced to stay. It can be carried forward gently... through objects, through shared experiences, through the quiet decision to notice what matters and give it form. There is care in that. A recognition that what we choose to preserve shapes what continues.

What remains is not accidental. It is shaped by attention... by care... by the willingness to make meaning visible so it does not disappear with time.

Zach also made me think differently about creativity.

Not as decoration... not as an addition... but as a way of leading. A way of building environments where people long to take part... where challenge and safety are not in opposition, but in conversation with each other. Where what is created holds something deeper than the moment itself.

Because connection is not a byproduct. It is the point.

Zach builds something else entirely... a world where the experience carries weight... where what happens stays with you... and where what you remember continues to shape you long after you leave.

. . .

Alyson Foisy

Player • Host

2025

Some conversations feel like interviews. This one felt like stepping into a room... the kind where energy is felt, where silence carries weight, where a person chooses her words with care because she understands they will last beyond the moment.

Alyson entered our conversation the way she plays... aware, grounded, and fully present. She does not rush toward easy answers. She pauses just long enough to reach something truer. There is both softness and steel in her. You feel it immediately. She will not reduce something meaningful just to make it easier to hold.

Before we moved into her story, we established something that matters more than most people realize. I explained how this process works... that our conversation would be recorded, transcribed, shaped, and returned to her for final approval. Nothing would be published without her consent. Nothing would move forward that did not feel true to her.

That kind of agreement changes how people speak. It creates safety. Necessary boundaries. Trust. It allows honesty to surface without fear of being mishandled.

Alyson understood that immediately. She also understood something else... the delicate balance between what is shared and what is protected. When I asked about the cast for her upcoming game, she answered with a quiet confidence. "It's secret," she said (as she should have) and then, with a soft laugh, she acknowledged what everyone in this world understands. Some things are hidden... and still known.

That tension lives at the center of these games and is precisely what makes them real.

◆

Alyson's story begins disappointment... the kind that lingers long after the moment itself has passed. Like so many players, she came into this world through love of the show. During the early months of a quiet and uncertain world, when routines disappeared and time stretched in unfamiliar ways, she found her way into online games. Strategy unfolded in conversation threads. Connection formed across distance. Something inside her recognized the rhythm immediately.

Her first live game felt close. Accessible. Something she could step into without hesitation.

And then it shifted.

She realized quickly that the game was asking something she had not yet learned how to give. "I was not the best liar," she told me, "nor did I know when people were lying to me." And when the vote came—sudden, unnecessary, and shaped by misjudgment—it did more than remove her from the game.

It unsettled her.

It is easy, from the outside, to dismiss moments like that. To call them part of the experience. To reduce them to something temporary. But inside the game, nothing feels temporary. Your body does not register it as fleeting. It registers as exclusion.

"I went out very unnecessarily in my very first game," she said, "and it left me with such anxiety." She did not go back the next day to watch the rest of the game unfold. She went home. She carried it.

And it stayed with her.

◆

There is a version of toughness that can easily be overlooked. It does not arrive fully formed. It reveals itself through repetition... through the decision to come back after something did not go the way you hoped it would. That is the version Alyson carries.

Her next LRG experience was different. The environment was new. The players were less experienced... and for the first time, she could feel her footing. She moved through challenges with confidence. She found what others missed. She held her own in ways that were no longer uncertain.

It was not dominance... it was recognition.

Alyson began to see that she could exist inside this space without apologizing for how she moved through it. And yet, what stayed with her most was not the success... it was the care.

When she spoke about one of her most meaningful experiences, she did not begin with placement or performance. She began with how she was treated.

She spoke about a host who saw players differently than most. "He is very thoughtful and caring about us as people, not just as pawns of a player," she said. And in that kind of environment, everything deepens. Connection feels more real. Disappointment feels sharper. Trust carries weight.

When you are seen as a person, not a pawn... the experience stops being abstract.

It becomes personal.

◆

Alyson understands something many players take time to learn. The qualities that serve you in life do not always protect you in the game. Her ability to connect, to communicate, to move easily between people... these are strengths. They are also signals. Visibility becomes risk. Presence becomes threat.

She described it with honesty and without complaint. "I am a confident person and I am friendly and make quick jokes, and I am not afraid to be myself in any of those ways," she said. "But in a game where you don't know who to trust or who to believe, or you're wanting to weed out threats... I think I seem pretty threatening."

And so she adapted.

Not by becoming someone else... but by recalibrating how much of herself she would allow others to see.

◆

When I asked why these games matter so deeply, Alyson did not dismiss the question. She acknowledged what is easy to say... that it is just a game. But she knew there was much more.

"When a game is done correctly," she said, "you are completely immersed in the experience and it becomes your entire world for that moment in time."

There is no outside noise. No distraction. No buffer between you and what you feel. Your body is tired. Your mind is alert. Your emotions are closer to the surface than they are in everyday life. Everything becomes immediate.

And in that environment... you see yourself clearly. Not a version you curate. Not a version you present. The version that stands when nothing else is available to hide behind.

For Alyson, that clarity brought something unexpected to the surface. Not weakness... but loneliness. Not the absence of people, but the absence of certainty. The absence of knowing, without question, that someone has chosen you above all others.

She identifies it without hesitation. The experience of moving through groups without feeling anchored.

The awareness that connection can exist without permanence.

The understanding that relying on yourself has been both her strength... and her protection.

"I don't think I've ever played in a game where I felt like I had somebody who was mine and I was theirs," she said quietly. "I am always relying on myself, getting myself through everything I do."

That kind of honesty does not come easily. It requires self-awareness. It requires courage. It requires the willingness to say something that many people feel… but rarely voice.

"I want to fricking win," she said, with the kind of certainty that leaves no room for doubt, "so I'm going to keep doing it until I get one."

◆

As our conversation moved toward its close, Alyson spoke about something that carries both weight and truth. The experience of being a woman in these spaces is not neutral. The physical realities are real. The discomfort, the lack of rest, the absence of ease… they do not disappear simply because the game has begun. The social realities are just as present. Assumptions form quickly. Strength is interpreted differently. Confidence is measured against expectation.

She thoughtfully considers what it means to adjust. "I am going to diminish myself in some way," she said plainly. Not because she believes she should, but because she understands what it might take. And then, with a laugh that carried both affection and edge: "…I'm willing to fade a little bit."

That calculation is not simple. It is not light. It is the kind of decision that reveals how much someone is willing to hold in order to move forward.

And then… just before we ended, something shifted.

She paused… and returned to something she said earlier to correct it.

She reminded herself… and me… that she is not without certainty. That she is not without someone who chooses her… and then she said, "I have my mother—I am not alone."

And in that moment, the room changed. Warmth replaced something heavier. Connection became visible again. I could see Alyson again the first day we met, admiring her thick red hair and confidence… and in the far off distant woods, Alyson's mother. There. Watching. And smiling.

◆

As we were wrapping up, Alyson's eyes widened, "Oh yeah... I'm going to host my first game this summer."

There is was, the full circle arc... the person who once left early, carrying disappointment and unanswered questions, is now the one entrusted to shape the experience for others.

Not to control it... but to hold it with care.

In her first confessional at *Surviving Bloomington*, she laughed at herself and said she wasn't a *mischief maker*, that maybe she'd just try to collect some keys.

She made mischief... and she definitely collected keys.

Keys she carries now... not to decide outcomes, but to protect the space where they unfold.

My Lens Reframed

Alyson is the epitome of endurance for me. I am in a season where I can choose where I place my energy... and I can see, more clearly than I would like, the moments where I step away too soon... when staying would ask more of me than I am ready to give.

Her story brings that into focus.

Grit is not always immediate. It is not always visible in the way we expect. Sometimes it is found in endurance... in the willingness to return and to continue engaging even when the experience does not resolve cleanly. There is something humbling in that kind of persistence... something that asks for more than instinct.

And over time, something else becomes visible.

A different kind of awe... one that reveals itself slowly... through consistency... through presence... through the decision to keep showing up.

What I see in Alyson is not a departure from who she is, but a refinement. A way of moving with greater awareness... without abandoning the core of herself in the process.

And it expands beyond her.

There is something powerful in the way she has moved from participant to host... from someone seeking belonging to someone who builds it. The experience changes when people are seen as whole... not as pieces to be moved. When care is present... the memory of a space carries something different.

What lingers is a woman who did not need to be chosen to belong... because she stayed long enough to become someone who creates belonging for others.

"I want to fricking win, so I'm going to keep doing it until I get one."

Rachel Rowe

Player

2026

"I'm 35, my body's changing all over again, but there's nothing quite like the change of the body with pregnancy and birth and the healing process after."

Rachel didn't come to me with a headline or a showy hook. She came with something rarer… *clarity*. We had spoken briefly after her vote out at *Survivor Indiana*, and the conversation stayed with her long after the cameras turned away. When we reconnected, it was not to relive the game. It was to name what the game revealed.

Rachel is one of the few mothers in this book, and that is noteworthy. Motherhood is a kind of constant giving that quietly reshapes our bodies, our identity, and our sense of self. When Rachel speaks, she does not posture. She reflects. She does not exaggerate. She tells the truth in grounded thoughts that land like stones dropped into still water, and from there the ripples begin to move outward in ways you can feel long after the moment passes.

What happens when a mother steps into the woods and asks, without apology, what her body, her mind, and her spirit can do now… for herself?

◆

Rachel is thirty-five. She is a mom, and she is honest about what many women whisper but rarely share. Pregnancy and birth change your body in ways you cannot fully prepare for until that season has arrived. There is the stretching and the healing, the tenderness and the fatigue, the strange moment of catching your reflection and wondering who you are now.

The slow realization that motherhood is sharing your body for a season... a place where someone else lives, feeds, grows, and heals, and when that season shifts, you are left to rediscover what is left.

"It's shared," she said. "It's a shared body and we push ourselves as moms. We'll do anything for our kids. But what if it's just you? How hard can you go for just you and no one else?"

The question hung in the air between us, and I realized it was not rhetorical. It was the question that brought her to the woods in the first place.

Rachel did not come to Live Reality Games believing she was strong. She came believing she was behind. She carried the quiet fear that she would be the one who could not keep up. What she found in the game was not a return to who she used to be. It was a new introduction to who she already was... capable, present, and sturdier than her inner critic had ever allowed her to believe.

◆

In the woods, without her phone and without the ability to *FaceTime*, without the familiar tether of constant updates, Rachel did something that felt almost radical for a modern mother.

She unplugged completely.

Rachel has traveled before. She trusts her husband, Caleb completely. She has support. But this was different. This was not a break with a soft landing. This was a break where the silence actually held, where the morning arrived without notifications, and where the world did not ask her to be needed every minute.

She described it simply.

"My kids aren't here. I don't have my phone. I'm completely unplugged... That alone was just such an impactful experience for me to really reflect: Hey, I'm a mom, but I'm also... this is something I love and I'm going to lean into that."

She kept returning to one question. What can my body do now? Not for her kids. Not for her household. Not for anyone else's comfort. Just for her.

It may sound selfish until you understand how much mothers disappear inside service. Rachel's language is not indulgent. It is reverent. She spoke about gratitude for her body as it is now, not as it used to be. Not perfect. Not untouched. Not younger.

But capable.

♦

Rachel told me about a hard moment from her season of *Surviving Bloomington*, one that still lives close to the surface. It was not a dramatic betrayal or a flashy blindside. It was words, and the way words can travel, shift, and land with more force than intended.

Somewhere in the chain of communication, a message reached Rachel.

Dead weight.

It was not necessarily meant as a personal attack, and she understood that. She could trace the miscommunication and see the game context. But understanding does not stop language from penetrating. When you already battle negative self-talk, an outside phrase can feel like confirmation. It can sound like the world finally agreeing with your worst private thoughts.

"Someone said I was dead weight," she told me, "and then I just started sobbing. Moments later I was being held."

One of the most human moments in her season had nothing to do with strategy. Mackenzi (Berg) wrapped Rachel in a sleeping bag and held her while she sobbed. There was no spectacle, just warmth around a person who needed it. Crinkling fabric, shared breath, and the kind of quiet care that makes the woods feel less like exposure and more like shelter.

Rachel chose not to crumble. She did not turn the moment into rage or revenge. She refused to let it make her smaller. She allowed it to become information. She let it sharpen her self-awareness, recognized the pull to spiral... and then, she resisted it.

What Rachel did next is the heart of this chapter.

She listened. *Even when it hurt.*

"I think that was the hardest point in that game... I knew the person mentioned didn't talk that way. Being able to listen and process, even when it hurt, was a real and powerful world experience."

There is a choice available to all of us when language arrives that presses on something already tender. We can choose anger. We can collapse inward. Or we can pause long enough to ask what is actually true.

Rachel paused... and that pause saved her game. More importantly, it revealed something about her own strength that she had not fully seen before.

♦

Behind the softness was a plan.

Part of Rachel's game was intentional invisibility. She wanted people to look past her, to assume she was a number, just a vote, just someone to drag along to the end.

Meanwhile, she was preparing her case.

"I used to be an English professor," she told me, and I could hear the smile in her voice. "So I'm like: here's my thesis, here's my evidence, here's my analysis... they won't know what hit them when I get to final tribal."

The woman who teaches story structure was building her own narrative arc in real time, drafting arguments in her mind while others assumed she was coasting. Rachel's strength is not boisterous. It is layered.

She reflected on what it cost her to give herself permission to play that way.

"You've got to be selfish to win," a friend told her before the game. And she took it in. "It was so hard to make selfish decisions."

After winning *Surviving Bloomington*, Rachel struggled to hold that permission. She had accepted that winning required a level of self-focus that did not come naturally to her, and afterward she questioned whether she was allowed to want it again.

It is a distinctly Rachel question. Not whether she could win again. But whether it was right for her to try.

♦

When I asked why we don't see more moms in this space, her answer held both truth and tenderness. She named the reality directly.

"I recognize it's a privilege to have a support system," she said. "I know that I would not have survived motherhood without some deep support."

Some mothers simply do not have that level of support. Others have it but hesitate to accept it. The guilt of leaving, even briefly, even when everything is genuinely okay, can be louder than the need. "If you have support," she said, "lean into it."

While a beach is beautiful, Rachel explained, the woods do something different. A vacation rests the body. An LRG asks the body and spirit to introduce themselves again. And for a mother who has poured herself into being needed, that introduction can change everything.

She also acknowledged the practical realities. Cost. Distance. Schedules. She deeply appreciates hosts who keep games accessible and who create scholarships and flexibility, *because those choices shape who gets to show up.*

In true Rachel fashion, she does not only participate. She invites others in. She finds herself telling strangers about LRGs, pulling up seasons on her phone, and encouraging people to try. She builds community while remaining fully herself.

♦

In fourth grade, Rachel's teacher read *Harry Potter and the*

Sorcerer's Stone aloud to the class. She immediately fell in love with story, with reading, and with the craft of *retelling*.

In fact, her master's thesis was on postmodern fairytale retellings. She has always been drawn to the question: *what happens when you take a familiar story and tell it in a way that makes visible what was hidden the first time.*

That is exactly what she does in the game. She takes what happens, the misread moments, the words that land wrong, the underestimation of a quiet woman planning her final tribal argument, and she tells the truest version of the story.

She is a *reteller*. She reframes without distorting.

Her faith shapes how she sees this. Being in the woods, for Rachel, is not just competitive. It is being inside something larger than herself, where filters fall away and people become who they are.

"Being in nature... for me, God's creation, there's just a real special opportunity there," she said. "The willingness to share things that maybe they hadn't ever shared before... there's a vulnerability that you get to experience out in the woods that can't really happen anywhere else."

While spirituality is a topic often left unexplored, Rachel spoke about the intersection of faith and gameplay with a clarity I deeply appreciated. She knows where her line is. Game lies exist to advance strategy. What she will not do is carry cruelty or use her gameplay to damage someone's dignity.

"There's gameplay," she said, "and then there's... hurting people. Are they hurt because they lost? That's something they can work through. Or are they hurt because you said or did something that crossed a line?"

She wants the difference between Rachel and Game-Rachel to be clear and known. Not as an excuse. As integrity.

Rachel and Caleb are in the process of becoming certified to foster, with hope of fostering to adopt. She spoke carefully, with full awareness of the weight of that decision. She wants their home to be truly safe... the kind of safe where a child can exhale and begin to rest.

She admitted the question many prospective foster parents quietly carry. Can I love a child who is not biologically mine? Then she answered it through lived experience.

"When you had just one child and you were pregnant with a second," she said, "how do our hearts love the same way? But somehow... our hearts are expanded, grown. I don't know how it works, but we're able to love." That is the pattern of Rachel's life. Expansion without applause.

She also shared something many women feel but rarely articulate. Sometimes the role of stay at home mom does not feel honored by the world. It does not come with titles or recognition, and often the reactions say more than the words.

I'm a stay at home mom, she said. They're like, what? And then she paused, as if weighing whether to say the next part. Sometimes the facial expressions... it doesn't get a certificate or a promotion.

Rachel is not ashamed. She is honest about the tension. She notices the pressure to qualify it.

I am a mom... *but...*

She is learning to release the "but" and stand in the fullness of what is true. She is a mom. That is enough, not because she lacks depth, but because she no longer needs to prove it.

At the close of our conversation, Rachel returned to what matters most. Her children. Negative self-talk has a way of repeating across generations, and she is paying attention.

In that space, it becomes clear why LRGs matter to her. They do not only test your body. They expose a need for validation and invite you to decide who gets to define you. "It strips everything away," she said, "so you can really see at your core who are you and what is true."

She is stronger than she believed. She wants her children to have opportunities to discover their own strength... strength rooted in truth rather than performance. She hopes they learn to listen well, to honor stories different from their own, and to recognize the humanity in others.

The world is overflowing with opinion and hungry for understanding, and Rachel, in her steady way, is building a life that answers that need.

My Lens Reframed

Rachel's chapter was pivotal as I waded through the depths of this book. She represents a form of growth that is not always celebrated in competitive spaces. Rachel reminds me that resiliency is its own kind of growth... especially when it is rooted in integrity.

Her story also expands the concept of who belongs in this community. Mothers are not symbols or categories. They are whole people carrying layered lives into these spaces. Motherhood changes the body, but it also changes how a person understands risk, courage, sacrifice, and worth. Rachel is not trying to escape her family. She is remembering herself within it.

As a storyteller, I am struck by the through line of her life. Her love for retelling fairytales is not incidental. It is a reflection of who she has always been. She is someone who searches for truth beneath the surface, who reframes without distortion, and who tells stories with care and intention. That instinct shaped how she moved through the game and how she now reflects on it.

And it deepens something in me as I sit with it.

Fortitude is not a single moment. It is an ongoing decision to return to truth when something distorted tries to take its place. To question the narratives we inherit... to examine the ones we carry... and to choose, again and again, what we allow to define us.

There is a deeper reckoning here... with the words we have absorbed and the meaning we have assigned to them. Words can wound. Care can hold. But healing begins in the moment we refuse to let a single experience define the whole of who we are.

My widened lens sees a woman learning to speak to herself with more honesty and more grace. A mother remembering that she still exists within the life she has built. A person choosing to see herself clearly... and to believe what she finds.

And that is beautiful... as is Rachel.

Unshakable... whole.

She walked into the woods wondering what she was capable of... and she walked out carrying something far more powerful...

A testament to who she has been all along.

Allen Yannone

Player • Host • Reality Retreat Owner

2024

"You're enough."

The house is quiet in the particular way homes become quiet when children have finally surrendered to sleep. The lights are low, the kind of soft evening glow that signals the day is winding down but not quite finished. Allen sits at his desk with the relaxed posture of someone used to late-night conversations, a small baby monitor resting beside his computer. I recall the soft hum of my own son's monitor and the way it carried the faint sounds of peaceful, soft breathing. And life.

In the middle of our conversation, Allen suddenly pauses and I see the monitor draw close to his ear, "Give me just a second," he says gently. "I hear my son."

There is no apology in his voice, no sense that he is interrupting something important. He simply stands and disappears from the frame for a moment. The conversation waits. The interview waits. The game, the stories, the strategy—all of it pauses while he goes to check on his son.

I wait. Imagining what he says... how he says it. I picture big sleepy eyes that settle the moment they see him and I smile.

A few minutes later Allen returns, settling back into his chair with the calm satisfaction of someone who knows exactly where he belongs.

Watching moments like this, I start to understand Allen in a way that has nothing to do with strategy. The games reveal something about him, yes, but they are not the center of his story. What becomes clear instead is something quieter and far more defining: Allen is a father... a family man first.

As our conversation unfolds, I wonder why we don't talk much about fatherhood in the LRG space (or *Survivor*). I wonder how fatherhood has impacted Allen and how he has grown since becoming?

◆

Our connection traces back through the web of this community, the way many of these stories do. In this world, introductions rarely happen directly. They move through people who become bridges, through shared games and overlapping histories. For Allen and me, that bridge is Eric.

Eric Eldredge was my cast-mate on *Surviving Bloomington,* but he was also the lead videographer for my very first live reality game—back when I was still learning what it meant to be watched while becoming someone new. When I later saw Eric's name on another cast list, I remember thinking with a sudden panic, *Oh no... he knows things...*

Not secrets exactly. Just the unguarded parts of yourself that surface when you are tired, hungry, unsure, and trying to navigate the complicated social terrain of a game that can ask you to be both loyal and strategic at the same time.

Allen laughs when I tell him this. "That's a good ally," he says.

And maybe that is the first thing to notice about Allen. He assumes connection before threat. You can see it in the way he listens, the way his eyes stay steady when someone else is speaking. Even before the first challenge begins, even before alliances start forming in quiet corners of the woods, Allen approaches the experience believing something meaningful can be built between people.

◆

Allen is thirty-five, which means *Survivor* has been woven into his life for almost as long as he can remember. He watched the very first season with his family. He still remembers the glimmer of the television in a dim living room, the ritual of Thursday nights when everyone gathered around the screen to watch something none of them yet fully understood. What caught Allen's attention even then was not just the survival elements or the competitions. It was behavior.

Who adapted? Who resisted? Who listened? Who waited? Winning, even back then, did not seem random to him. It felt layered.

His first step into the broader reality game world didn't happen outdoors. It happened online during the pandemic when a friend asked if he would fill a spot in a weekend ORG played over Zoom. Allen said yes without knowing much about what he was agreeing to. That is often how these stories begin—with curiosity before clarity.

He loved it immediately. Strategy unfolded in chat windows and timed votes. Alliances formed through typed messages and quick decisions. The tension was real even through a screen. But somewhere along the way he learned something that changed everything: people weren't just playing these games online. They were playing outside.

They were sleeping on the ground, competing in the elements, building challenges in the woods and lighting fires under open skies. The dream he had watched for years on television suddenly had a physical form. Sweat replaced screen glow. Firelight replaced Wi-Fi.

And that is where Kadie enters the story—not as a supporting character but as a partner in the adventure.

Allen and Kadie discovered *Can You Survive?* together, and the host cast them both while keeping their marriage secret from the rest of the players. It was Allen's first live game, and he describes it with the kind of honesty that only comes from reflection.

He was messy.

Too many alliances. Too many promises whispered under trees. Too many conversations happening at once in the thick summer air.

He and Kadie were both voted out early.

For many players, that moment becomes the end of the story. It becomes the reason they decide the games are not for them after all.

For Allen, it became information. "I needed a reset," he tells me. "I needed to figure out what I did wrong."

There is no shame in the way he says it. Only curiosity.

Some people lose and shrink.

Some people lose and study.

As I listened to Allen describe his response, I decided that Allen is the portrait of what it looks like when a person invites adventure and growth into their life.

Not the version people talk about easily, the inspirational kind that fits neatly into a speech. The real kind. The version that asks you to examine your mistakes, to return after failure, to choose learning over pride again and again.

Allen seems to move through the world routinely practicing this.

He returned and won his second *Survivor*-format LRG. Then he won again, this time in a *Blood vs. Water* season. Two wins out of three games is the kind of record that invites people to build a legend around someone. Allen resists that entirely. When he talks about those wins, he doesn't sound triumphant.

He sounds analytical. Winning, for him, is not the finish line. It is a data point.

When I ask him what separates a good game from a great one, he doesn't talk about flashy blindsides or dramatic speeches. Instead he talks about ownership. He remembers watching a final tribal council where a player answered every question with calm conviction. There was no rewriting of history, no attempt to soften difficult decisions.

Yes, I did that. And here is why. No flinching. No scrambling to be liked.

Then he describes his own winning game in contrast ... quieter, more patient. Instead of forcing strategy outward, he let people come to him. He listened longer than he spoke. He watched how the room moved, how personalities shifted, how alliances formed and dissolved beneath the surface. And then, when the timing was right, he tipped one domino.

The rest followed naturally. "A great game isn't loud," he tells me. "It's structured."

♦

Later in our conversation, Allen says something that lingers with me long after the call ends. He describes these games as theater—not scripted and not fake, *but improvised*. Everyone is performing in some way, adapting their role moment by moment. The forest becomes a stage. The fire becomes a spotlight. The jury becomes the audience.

And sometimes the audience decides your story is over.

♦

As we move into heavier subjects like the emotional toll of being voted out, Allen never dismisses the weight of that experience. He explains that, yes, it is a game—but it is also a mirror. Out there in the woods, people say things they have never said out loud before. Hunger and exhaustion dissolve the polite layers we carry through everyday life. Vulnerability accelerates. Then a vote happens.

When I ask what lesson he carries with him, his answer is almost disarmingly simple. "You're enough."

Not if you win. Not if you place well. Not if you're chosen.

You're enough regardless. Sometimes you simply weren't part of someone else's plan.

A vote is not a verdict.

Feel it. Grieve it. Learn from it.

Then let it go.

For players who already carry histories of exclusion—LGBTQ players, marginalized players, anyone who has spent years wondering if they belong—that vote can echo in places far older than the game itself.

Allen understands that. Not with judgment. With care.

You hear that same care in his voice when he talks about watching Kadie play. The pride arrives before the analysis. He tells me about watching her compete in *Survival Challenge* and her first night ever sleeping outside ... and the way it rained. He imagined the cold ground, the damp clothes, and the exhaustion that follows a sleepless night in unfamiliar conditions.

Then morning came.

Kadie stepped into the new day with damp hair, bright eyes, and a smile that made it clear she was ready for whatever came next. "She was just... ready," Allen says ... and the way he says it holds something unmistakable.

Love.

Not the quiet kind that stays in the background. The kind that steps back full of pride and says, *look at her go.*

As the conversation winds down, the pattern becomes impossible to miss. Allen studies his games, but he also studies himself. The same curiosity that leads him to ask how he could have played a move better also shows up in the rest of his life. How can I listen better here? How can I show up more fully there?

Growth, for Allen, is not a project he completes once and moves on from. It is the way he moves through the world.

And it's inspiring.

MY LENS REFRAMED

Allen altered the way I think about continued growth. Most people talk about it after they have already arrived somewhere they are proud of. He moves toward it earlier... when it is still unfinished... still uncomfortable... still uncertain. He welcomes the feedback, the discomfort, the second attempt.

Watching him brought something into focus for me... growth is not swift. It is something you choose... again and again.

And that choice rarely looks like progress in the way we expect.

Growth, in his world, is not something you arrive at. It is something you return to... often in the moments that feel least like movement. It lives in the willingness to look closely at what did not work... not with judgment, but with curiosity. To treat loss not as failure, but as information... something that sharpens rather than diminishes.

There is a discipline in that kind of reflection... but it is not rigid. It is open. It asks more of you, not less. It requires an honesty that ego resists... and a humility that most people avoid.

And over time, something begins to build.

Not perfection... but awareness. The kind that allows a person to keep becoming... long after others have decided they are finished growing.

Allen does not wait to arrive somewhere he can be proud of.

He chooses growth... before that.

And then again... and again... and again.

WORDS OF WISDOM

A vote is not a verdict.
Feel it. Grieve it. Learn from it.
Then let it go.

~ Allen Yannone

The trail is never walked in isolation,
even when it feels that way.
Long before our arrival,
someone has already stood where we stand…
already faced what we are trying to understand.
Their choices linger in ways we cannot always see,
shaping the ground beneath us,
steadying us when we do not yet know we need it.
We enter as individuals,
carrying our own stories,
our own fears,
our own reasons.
At first, it feels like something we must navigate alone…
something to prove,
something to endure.
But slowly, almost without noticing,
the terrain begins to soften.

Part Two
Community Is Built with Intention

Belonging may begin with courage, but it survives because someone builds the room. Every fire pit, every challenge, every safe landing exists because someone chose to carry responsibility. Care is not accidental. It is designed. Structure is not restrictive. It is protective. The chapters in this section honor those who learned that community requires intention — and that leadership is often quiet, unseen, and relentless.

"Am I ready to carry this again?"

~ Chris Lord

John Vataha
LRG Pillar

2024

What does it look like when a dream refuses to stay contained... when it grows beyond the person who first carried it and becomes something others can stand inside?

John does not tell the story of *Survival Challenge* as if he is recounting a triumph. He tells it like someone still slightly astonished that it worked at all... like someone who understands just how close it came to unraveling before it ever had the chance to become real. There is humor in the way he remembers it, a kind of disbelief woven through the details. Nobody got arrested. Nobody got hypothermia. Nobody ended up on the evening news. The way he says it feels less like exaggeration and more like gratitude... as if the early days required just enough grace to hold together what logic alone could not.

The story does not begin in Maine. It begins earlier, in 2008, when John found himself in Samoa, standing close enough to the machinery of *Survivor* to feel its pulse. There is a difference between watching something and touching it. In Samoa, he crossed that line. He felt the weight of the props. He heard the hum of production. He witnessed the precision behind what millions would later see edited into something seamless. That moment did not create the dream. It confirmed it. What he had been drawn to was not imagined. It was real... structured, intentional, and alive.

That confirmation followed him home.

In New York, at a finale event filled with energy and recognition, he stepped into a different kind of space. Hotel lobbies turned into gathering points. People clustered together with a kind of shared language that did not need explanation. They spoke in terms of blindsides and idols, of moments that only made sense if you had been paying attention long enough to understand what was at stake beneath the surface. He calls them crazy people with affection, not distance... people who do not simply watch the game, but orbit it, shape their time around it, and carry it with them.

That is where he first heard about the *Houston Reality Challenge*.

He applied. He played. And for someone who had loved *Survivor* from a distance, it felt like stepping onto sacred ground. Fans and former players sharing space. Challenges unfolding in real time. The line between spectator and participant dissolving. It was everything he thought it might be.

And still... something in him asked for more.

There is a moment that comes when experience no longer satisfies curiosity. It sharpens it. Houston was not a conclusion. It was a beginning. It revealed what was possible, and in doing so, it created a different kind of question... what would this look like if it went deeper?

John did not want a version of the game that could be replicated easily. He wanted something that could be felt. Less park, more wilderness. Less imitation, more embodiment. He wanted a space where hunger meant something, where exhaustion was not simulated, where the environment itself became part of the experience. He wanted the game to breathe.

The problem was simple.

He did not have the land.

So he did what people do when the vision outgrows the available resources... he kept imagining anyway. He and Steve Pickett talked about possibilities that did not yet exist. They spoke about land not as a business plan, but as an opening. The kind of conversation that lives somewhere between unrealistic and inevitable.

Then something shifted.

At *Hearts of Reality*, Bob Crowley entered the conversation. When John described what he was trying to build, Bob did not hesitate. He offered something tangible. One hundred acres in Maine. It was not a negotiation. It was an opening. A sentence that carried weight because it turned vision into possibility.

That is the moment the idea found its footing.

From there, things began to move. Family became involved. Dates were chosen. October 2013. Season One. There was no system to support it. No structured casting process. No social media engine to gather attention. There were only conversations, phone calls, and a willingness to move forward without certainty.

"We literally said, we have two main goals for season one," he told me. "Let's not get anybody killed and let's not embarrass ourselves." That was the bar. That was the entire plan.

What followed was something far less controlled than anyone would have designed if they had known what they were doing.

The property that was meant to serve as a base was not fully secured. Flights arrived late. Darkness fell faster than expected. There was no electricity to rely on, no infrastructure to lean into when things began to shift. Contestants were hidden in separate spaces, instructed not to speak. Production moved through the night trying to locate people who were following the rules too well to be found.

Names were called into the dark.

Silence answered.

Eventually, sixteen blindfolded individuals were gathered and placed onto a hay cart. The road stretched ahead of them, uneven and uncertain. The air carried cold that had not been accounted for. The sky held no light to guide them. Somewhere in that moment, Bob turned to John with a question that lives at the edge of every untested idea.

"What are we going to say to the sheriff when he pulls us over?"

The cart got stuck in mud. Campsites were harder to find than expected. The night dropped into a cold that settled into the body. Breath became visible. Hands lost feeling. The ground offered little comfort. The experience had already begun before anyone could fully prepare for it.

Morning arrived with a single hope... that everyone was still there.

"I'm just standing there in the field just counting," he said, "praying that we get to 16 and everyone looks relatively upright."

They were.

Sixteen people, still standing.

Something had held.

From that moment forward, *Survival Challenge* carried something distinct. It was not a replication. It was not a tribute. It was something rooted in the same spirit, but shaped by different conditions. *Survivor* players were present from the beginning, not as an addition, but as part of the foundation. Over time, that connection deepened. Players refined their understanding of the game in John's space. Others returned to it after feeling unseen elsewhere, rediscovering something they thought they had lost.

This was not fandom.

It was restoration.

At some point, John stopped applying to *Survivor*. Not because the love faded. The love matured. Time has a way of clarifying what belongs and what does not. The body changes. Life expands. Priorities shift. And sometimes, after chasing something long enough, a quieter truth emerges... the thing you were seeking has already begun to take shape in another form.

"It's kind of become the replacement for what I thought *Survivor* was going to be for me," he said simply.

Creating became the answer.

Hosting became the fulfillment.

What he had once hoped to find, he began to build.

As the game grew, so did its demands. What started as something small began to stretch. More players. More days. More complexity. The details multiplied. Equipment. Volunteers. Logistics that required attention at every level. The dream did not disappear under that weight. It adapted. It learned how to stand.

With growth came something else... responsibility. Charity became part of the structure. Then came a broader awareness that the community itself required care. Diversity, access, collaboration. These were not abstract ideas. They were necessary components of something that was expanding quickly.

He spoke about the lesson that growth eventually teaches every builder.

"When it's your baby," he said, "it's got a certain flavor. And then as it gets bigger, you welcome the help... but not always the suggestions."

John began to speak about the ecosystem. Not ownership. Not control. Direction. A clear vision. An ecosystem cannot be forced into uniformity. It must be supported in a way that allows it to grow without losing what makes it alive. He understood that strength would come from connection, not consolidation.

When I asked him what mattered most, what he would not want overlooked, he did not mention the scale of the game or the complexity of its design. He spoke about community. The people who gather before the game begins. The feeling of arriving somewhere that holds familiarity and competition at the same time. The way relationships form, fracture, and then find their way back to something shared. The way belonging outlasts the moment of being voted out.

That is what he built.

◆

At the center of it all is something quieter, something that began long before Maine or Houston or any structured version of the game.

It began with his daughter.

"*Survivor* comes out, I'm a single dad, my daughter's nine years old," he said. "It is interwoven into our relationship... She's thirty-three now. So it's twenty-four years of this."

She filmed his audition tapes. She stood beside him in the early stages. She became part of the process before there was a process to understand. Over time, she grew into the role of production manager. The story did not stay fixed in one generation. It expanded.

The game did not end.

It evolved.

Survival Challenge did not begin polished. It did not begin with certainty. It began with something far more important... honesty. The imperfections were not flaws. They were an authentic indication that something real was being attempted.

And that attempt became a foundation.

My Lens Reframed

John challenged me to reconsider what it actually means to build something that lasts.

Not just to start it... not just to shape it in the beginning... but to stay with it long enough to watch it change. To let it become something that no longer reflects only you... but the people who begin to find themselves inside it.

There is an unspoken restraint in that. A willingness to release control... not because the vision no longer matters, but because it has grown beyond what one person can hold. That kind of trust is rare... to build something with intention and then allow it to take on a life that is no longer yours alone.

And it deepens the definition of courage.

Not just the courage to begin... but the courage to loosen your hold. To trust that what was created can sustain itself... even as it shifts... even as it becomes something you could not have fully anticipated.

There is also a responsibility in that kind of creation. Not just to build... but to tend. To protect the conditions that allow something meaningful to continue... long after the moment of its beginning has passed.

Because not everything we build is meant to stay ours.

Some things are meant to take root... to grow beyond their origin... to be shaped by the people who enter them and find something of themselves inside.

What began simply does not stay small.

It becomes something no longer defined by where it started...
but by all the lives that now exist within it.

NIKKI NEISES
PLAYER • WORLD-BUILDER

2024

"I didn't just want to run a game... I wanted to build a world."

Nikki did not stumble into the Live Reality Game world. She studied it long before she ever touched the ground. As a child watching *Survivor*, her attention moved differently. The drama was there, but it was never what held her. She was drawn to the design. Season two lit something that never quieted. She watched how trust formed and fractured, how alliances shifted not only through words but through timing, how production built tension without allowing chaos to overtake the structure. While others watched for blindsides, Nikki watched for systems. She paid attention to how votes stacked, how power moved quietly before it declared itself, how the shape of the game influenced the behavior inside it.

By the time she turned eighteen, she was not waiting to be cast. She was already practicing. Her first real game happened online, a months-long *Survivor*-style ORG she found because she dared to post an audition video to *YouTube*. That single decision carried her further than she expected. She made it to the final two and lost by a single vote. Loss has a way of clarifying what matters. That experience did not simply teach Nikki how to play. It taught her how people feel inside a game. She began to understand how bitterness forms in the quiet spaces between alliances, how loyalty fractures when timing slips, and the way power moves long before it is named. Something deeper took hold in that moment... something more enduring than strategy.

She was hooked.

For years, Nikki lived inside online *Survivor*-style and B*ig Brother*-style ORGs, sometimes five at once. Screens glared late into the night. Conversations layered across multiple chats. Alliances formed and dissolved in parallel. Strategy built on strategy until the mental load became constant. She learned quickly. Her instincts sharpened. She understood how to move through complex social systems with precision. Over time, that pace began to take something from her. The same intensity that made her effective also made it unsustainable. Eventually, she stepped away, not because she had lost interest, but because she understood that stepping back was the only way to return differently.

When Live Reality Games began to emerge as something physical and immersive, she recognized the shift immediately. The next evolution would not live on a screen. It would live in the body.

Her first in-person experience at *Surviving Reelfoot* ended early. She was the second person voted out, a result that surprised her more than she expected. On paper, she carried experience. Years of gameplay. Refined instincts. Strategic awareness. Live Reality Games required something else entirely. Presence could not be filtered. Energy could not be edited. Nerves could not be hidden behind a screen. There was no logging off, no buffer between reaction and consequence. There was only the environment... the wind in the trees, the ground beneath her feet, the conversations that lingered long after comfort had left.

Even after being voted out, Nikki stayed. She remained in the woods and watched production with the same attention she had once given to gameplay. Her focus shifted toward structure. She noticed where transitions slowed the experience, where communication broke down, where stronger systems could protect both players and the integrity of the game itself. She saw what worked, and she saw what did not. More importantly, she saw what was missing.

When she asked to help with future seasons, the answer was no. That moment could have closed something. Instead, it planted a seed. "From that point," she said simply, "I was like—I can do this on my own."

If the space would not make room for her, she would build one that did.

◆

Survive did not begin with scale or formal planning. It began in a pool. "I was in my dad's pool," she told me. "Me, my cousin Laine, and two other girlfriends—one who actually played *Reelfoot* with me—and we were sitting there and we're like, we could do *Survivor* here. And then we started brainstorming ideas. It started from this little core group of four women and we just made it happen."

On her father's property in McHenry, Illinois, surrounded by waterfalls and stonework shaped over years of craftsmanship, the idea found its ground. Her uncle Mike brought construction expertise. Her cousin Laine brought trust. Nikki brought vision and a refusal to compromise what she believed the experience could be. *Survive* was never intended to replicate *Survivor*. It was meant to honor it by building something that could stand on its own.

Season One proved the concept. Structures rose from sketches drawn by hand. Challenges moved from idea to blueprint to physical form. Systems were tested in real time. The game began to take shape in a way that could be felt, not just imagined. Season Two expanded that vision, pushing beyond what had already been proven.

The helicopter arrived as an extension of that mindset. It was not spectacle for its own sake. It was an offering. "This is honestly one of my favorite moments ever," she said. "I hear it, and I'm like, bring in the chopper. And everyone's like, *ha ha*, good joke. And I'm like, it's for you. And they're like, *ha ha, ha ha*. And I'm like, seriously, it's for you."

She paused. "Just to see their faces—it was such a magical moment that I'll never forget. That I was able to give that experience to these people."

Nikki understood that shared awe creates shared memory, and shared memory deepens connection. Wind moved across faces. What began as disbelief turned into realization. This was real. Laughter broke through. Families shared the sky. For a moment, the game loosened its grip, and something else took its place.

Wonder.

That moment carried beauty, and it also carried consequence. Complaints followed. Permits became obstacles. The property that had made the vision possible could no longer hold the game. Creation often invites resistance. Nikki absorbed that lesson fully.

Building *Survive* tested her creativity, but running it tested her leadership in ways she had not yet encountered. Season One brought a co-host who failed to carry the weight of the role. Harmful language surfaced. Instability grew. When he left mid-season, the responsibility did not disappear. It shifted entirely onto her.

"When I stepped in and started being a host," she said, "it was like—okay, well I can do this. And it's not that I fully doubted myself, but I did. Because I hadn't done it. So from then on I'm like, okay, *no*. This is my game. I'm going to host it... I hold the vision for it."

Nikki stepped forward without hesitation. She hosted, recalibrated, reassigned, and stabilized the experience in real time. Players continued to move through the game, often unaware of the full weight she was carrying behind the scenes. Leadership revealed itself in that moment as something far more demanding than vision. It required presence under pressure, clarity in uncertainty, and the willingness to hold the structure together when it began to fracture.

By Season Two, the system had evolved. Production was no longer informal. Roles were defined. Communication was structured. Expectations were clear.

"I now have a production team of forty people," she said, "and that's a lot of people to manage. So having structure and having the right people in leadership roles was very important." She laid it out clearly: a leader in media, a leader in each area, everyone reporting upward. "Having the right people in leadership roles allowed me to become the host during the game."

Nikki did not simply create a game. She built infrastructure, and that decision allowed everything else to stand.

Her work exists within a space where very few women are building at that scale. That reality is not separate from how she leads. It informs the way she designs for safety without diminishing intensity, the way she holds both care and competition in the same space without forcing them into opposition. She does not chase chaos. She shapes experience. She does not confuse control with leadership. She understands that structure is what allows creativity to endure, and that care is not a secondary element of the game.

It is part of what makes the game worth playing. "When you ask other people," she said, reflecting on what she's learned, "the vision is yours. You can't ask other people to execute your vision."

That realization did not arrive with bitterness. It arrived with a sweet surrender. She is the one who sees it. She is the one who holds it. And she is the one who is best equipped to build it into something others can step inside and be changed.

And that is exactly what Nikki build. In doing so, she created a space where people do more than participate. They step into a world designed especially for them—and to give them a lasting experience.

My Lens Reframed

What stayed with me after sitting with Nikki was not just what she built... but her desire to build for those who would experience it. There is also a difference between having an idea and taking responsibility for it. She did not wait to see if something like this would exist. She became the person to design it... and then continued, long after the excitement of beginning had passed.

It made me think about how often vision is treated like inspiration... something fleeting, something optional. What I see in her asks more. It asks for consistency... for protection... for a kind of care that does not disappear when things become difficult.

Some things do not exist until someone decides they must.

And once they do... they require more than imagination to survive (pun intended). They require attention... a willingness to hold something steady when others only see the finished experience. The kind of leadership that lives in decisions most people never notice... but feel in every detail of what they step into.

She did not just imagine something meaningful.

She built long enough to make sure it held.

And there is something else in that... something quieter, but just as powerful.

A responsibility that is not measured by recognition... but by what continues to exist... what continues to hold... even when the creator is no longer at the center.

Because the most meaningful things we experience are often carried by someone who chose not to let them disappear.

Nikki did not wait for a place to exist.

She built it.

Kc Winnecke
Player • Creator • Host

2024

"I had to fail a couple times before I understood what I was actually looking for."

Some people chase a dream until it exhausts them. Kc Winnecke held his long enough to let it transform.

He was seven years old when *Survivor* first aired... young enough to be mesmerized by the spectacle, old enough to sense that something deeper was unfolding beneath it. He remembers the flicker of firelight on the television screen. The quiet tension that settled just before a vote. The pull was never the prize. The pull was the structure. The way pressure revealed people. The way invisible rules formed between strangers when comfort disappeared and choice began to carry consequence.

While other kids reenacted challenges, Kc studied patterns. He noticed who spoke first and who waited. He watched who survived not by strength, but by perception. Story mattered to him early, not as performance, but as truth. He paid attention to how moments were framed, how decisions were remembered, how meaning could be clarified or distorted depending on who held the lens.

For years, that fascination narrowed into a singular dream. *Survivor.* Over time, the dream began to press too hard.

By his early twenties, the pursuit had taken on weight. Casting cycles passed. Applications blurred together. The dream that once felt electric began to feel evaluative. Each near miss made the goal feel both closer and further away at the same time. The question shifted. It was no longer, *would I be good?* And became *Am I enough.*

What saved Kc was not abandoning the dream.

It was refusing to let it consume him.

Surviving Bloomington did not begin with scale or certainty. It began with a question.

What if...

He asked a small group of friends if they wanted to play a homemade version of *Survivor* in the woods. There were no cameras. No sponsors. No legacy to protect. Just borrowed supplies and curiosity. He expected something loose. Something temporary. A weekend experiment that would dissolve as quickly as it began.

Instead, everyone showed up.

Participation gave way to commitment. Shoes sank into damp soil. Conversations sharpened under the canopy of trees. Strategies formed in real time. When the first torch was snuffed, when smoke rose into the evening air, something shifted.

Silence followed.

Not the kind of silence that feels uncertain... the kind that feels reverent.

Kc recognized it immediately, even though he didn't have words for it yet, the depth was undeniable. The moment someone wants to stay and someone else has to leave, everything clarifies. Behavior sharpens. Truth surfaces. The game stops being an idea and becomes an experience.

One player, Cassandra Bots, would later give language to what he had sensed. The game gave her something she had not realized she was missing. Not attention. Not approval.

Confirmation.

Confirmation that she was not simply being tolerated.

She was being chosen.

That realization was not contained to the woods. It followed her home. It reshaped how she understood herself in rooms that had once felt uncertain.

Kc understood then that he had not created entertainment.

He had created an *experience*.

As seasons continued, the scale expanded. Friends became applicants. Applicants became travelers. Donations grew. *Surviving Bloomington* evolved into a nonprofit, raising tens of thousands of dollars for homelessness services provided through the *Shalom Community Center* in Bloomington, Indiana.

Growth was never the point.

Intention was.

Kc did not design the game to help people escape reality. He designed it to help them encounter it more honestly. Conversations about identity were welcomed rather than avoided. Pronouns were honored with care. Language was chosen with authenticity. Safety was not something added after harm occurred... it was built into the structure from the beginning.

It was never about creating something flawless for Kc.

It was about creating something honest.

Behind the scenes, his editorial instinct became just as defining as his design. Hours of footage were not simply assembled. They were shaped. Confessionals were placed in context. Story arcs were clarified with intention and meaning was revealed.

People were not reduced to characters or pawns for ratings.

They were allowed to be human.

Eventually, Kc stepped into the arena he had built.

His first experience as a player followed a familiar pattern. Bold decisions. Assertive strategy. A confidence that read as control. The loss that followed carried clarity. The jury was bitter. The feedback was unmistakable, even when it was unspoken. Dominance without care rarely survives reflection.

The second game deepened the lesson. This time, he was surrounded by players who read him quickly. His instincts did not land the same way. Conversations shifted without him fully registering it. Luck carried him further than intention. When he was voted out, there was nothing left to explain away.

The third game became the turning point. He did not enter to prove anything. He entered to contribute. Listening replaced over-speaking. Trust replaced leverage. Attention expanded beyond the game to include the people inside it.

That was the season he won.

Not because he mastered manipulation... but because he mastered presence.

Surviving Bloomington has never been rigid. Kc describes it as a living system. Structured, but responsive. Planned, but attentive. The game shifts with the people inside it. It expands when it needs to. It contracts when it must. It listens.

Mistakes are acknowledged. Adjustments are made. Feedback is treated as information. Authenticity matters more than perfection.

This is why the game does not feel like a production.

It feels like an arena.

Alive. Demanding. Human.

Kc's vision extends beyond what already exists. He imagines Live Reality Games as something larger. A developing sport. Seasons that connect. Regional identity. Players recognized not only for how far they go, but for how they play and how they treat others across time.

In that vision, *Survivor* is not replaced.

It is the championship.

◆

Kc did not stop wanting *Survivor*. He stopped needing it to define him. That shift changed everything.

He built something that gives others what he once longed for. A place to be seen. A place to be challenged. A place to belong. A place where meaning is not manufactured, but discovered.

Dreams do not disappear when they evolve.

They deepen.

My Lens Reframed

There are some people in this work who did not just contribute to the story... they made the story possible.

Kc is one of them.

Before there were interviews... before there was language to hold what I was witnessing... there was a space he helped shape. A place where people could arrive, not just to play, but to be seen... to be known... to experience something that felt larger than the structure of a game.

Sitting with him, I began to understand what happens when ambition grows into something more. The desire to be seen does not disappear... it expands. It becomes a responsibility to see others clearly...

to build something that allows them to experience themselves differently inside it.

And that kind of work is not accidental.

Culture is shaped... often quietly... by the decisions no one sees. What is encouraged. What is protected. What is allowed to take root. Over time, those choices become the structure people move inside... the difference between performing belonging and actually feeling it.

What he created was not just an environment.

It was a beginning.

And what stays with me is the dedication and committment inside that beginning. Storytelling, at its best, is not only about what is remembered... it is about how people come to understand themselves within the experience. When it is done with care, it does more than reflect a moment.

It reshapes it.

Kc did not stop at the game.

He widened it... and created something that could hold more than competition.

It could hold people.

Shaw Ashley
Player • Creator

2024

"I learned quickly... you can't do it alone, and you're not supposed to."

I met Shaw the way you meet certain people in this community... not through a formal introduction, but through the ripple of something he created. His name surfaced first in passing, attached to a game, then to a role, then to a presence that felt far more established than it should have been for someone his age. There was already weight there, already structure, already something working behind the scenes. And then I saw him in motion, not presenting himself, not trying to prove anything, but simply doing the work that needed to be done.

There is a difference between someone who wants to lead and someone who already has. You can feel it before you can name it. Shaw moved through the space with a steadiness that did not ask for permission. Tables were set. Materials were organized. Questions were answered before they turned into confusion. Adults twice his age responded to him not because he demanded authority, but because he carried it naturally. That was the moment I understood that what makes Shaw different is not his age. It is the way he has already decided that leadership is something you step into, not something you wait to be handed.

His story begins in a time when the world felt smaller. When movement slowed and the spaces that once held energy and connection grew quiet. Camps closed. Programs paused. Children stayed inside. And while many people adjusted to that stillness, Shaw resisted it in a way that did not look like rebellion, but like vision.

"Covid was just starting and all of the summer camps that my little brother would go to were shutting down," he told me. "All the kids were forced to stay inside the house and I hated it. I wanted everybody to get outside and just keep going."

He did not want things to return to normal. He wanted something alive again. He wanted kids outside, moving, competing, laughing, finding their way back to one another in a way that could not be replicated through a screen.

What he understood, even then, was that belonging is not something you wait for. It is something you build.

So he built it.

He took what he loved about *Survivor*—not as entertainment but as structure, as language, as a way of bringing people together through shared experience—and he translated it into something real. Not theoretical. Not scaled down in intention. Real in the way that requires planning, responsibility, and follow through. Children arrived unsure of what they were stepping into. Parents watched carefully, measuring whether this would hold. And then the game began. Tribes formed. Challenges ran. Stories unfolded in real time. And what Shaw created was not just a camp. It was an experience that returned something to those kids that had been taken from them... movement, connection, and the simple joy of being part of something together.

As the experience grew, so did the need to support it. Vision alone could not carry what he was building. It needed structure, resources, and belief from others. And when the idea surfaced to invite people into the experience in a new way, Shaw did what builders do. He reached out. He asked. He refined. He tried again when the answer was not immediate. He did not approach it with entitlement. He approached it with clarity.

"In January, Sandra was like, absolutely not," he said, laughing. "I don't know what this is. I'm not involved. I'm onto bigger and better things." He paused. "I was like, I'm going to try again. I feel like if I explained it to her enough, maybe." He reached out again in March. Then came the unexpected: a Facebook Messenger video call. "I'm like, oh my God, this has got to be a butt dial. And she's like, *Hello Shaw*." An hour-long FaceTime. And the next morning, a message. She was in.

When the door opened, it did more than validate his effort. It expanded what was possible. It allowed others to see what he had already been building, not as a small, local idea, but as something with gravity. And Shaw met that moment with the same posture he had from the beginning. He did the work. He stayed steady. He allowed the experience to grow without losing its center.

By the second season, something had shifted. Not just in scale, but in connection. People did not simply arrive and leave. They stayed in conversation. They carried the experience with them. Relationships formed that extended beyond the structure of the game itself. There is something powerful about that kind of environment, where people are brought together through challenge and choice and leave with something that continues to matter after it ends.

◆

Shaw understands that these games are not only about competition. They are about exposure. They reveal how people show up when things are uncertain, when they are tired, when they are asked to make decisions that carry weight. They reveal what people hold onto and what they let go of. And because he understands that, he builds with care.

"I look at it two ways," he said. "There are a lot of people in these games who just feel like they've lost their opportunity—who have applied for twenty-four years and feel like it's never going to happen, or they're too unique, they'll never be cast. And this is their outlet. They save up money every year just to do this and meet people." He let that settle. "This gives them that one opportunity they never thought they could do. And it is powerful."

There has always been a teacher in him. That instinct did not begin here. It simply found its expression here. A desire to create environments where people can step into something and be changed by it. And as he stepped further into that role, he learned what all leaders eventually learn—that vision is only the beginning. Sustaining something requires trust. It requires letting go of the idea that you can hold everything yourself.

◆

There is a quiet moment in his story where that realization takes shape. He entered his first season prepared to manage every detail. And then, in the middle of it, he saw clearly that he could not be everywhere at once. Instead of forcing it, he adjusted. He asked for help. He expanded the system. That decision did not diminish what he had built. It allowed it to become stronger.

That growth did not come without friction.

"The biggest thing I ran into was people not taking me seriously because of my age," he said. "And that really disappointed me. I believed in myself and I knew I could do it." He paused before adding: "Had you not known my age, you probably would've thought I was an adult. And you probably wouldn't have even looked at it two different ways."

That is the kind of leadership that does not announce itself, but proves itself over time. Around him, there were people who believed in what he was doing. Family who supported him. Volunteers who showed up. And then there were those who stepped in not just to appear, but to work alongside him. For Shaw, that was Meredith Chandler—his high school math teacher and friend who became his co-host. He understood the significance: when someone with experience chooses to invest in something you are creating, it is not accidental. It is recognition.

◆

When Shaw speaks about the future of this community, he does not speak from a place of ego. He speaks from a place of care. He understands that growth brings complexity. That as something expands, it becomes harder to protect what made it meaningful in the first place. And still, he believes in it.

"*Survivor*'s been on for twenty-five years," he said. "We don't know how much longer we're going to have it. So this is what's going to be the legacy of *Survivor*—to continue it on. We have to hold onto this and come together and make it happen so we can continue to enjoy *Survivor* for years to come in this world."

That belief is not theoretical. It is already happening... and Shaw has been part of building it since the summer he refused to let things stay quiet.

MY LENS REFRAMED

With Shaw, I found myself reconsidering when leadership actually begins.

There is a quiet assumption many hold... that it comes later. After enough experience. After enough proof. After someone else tells us we are ready.

He does not wait for that.

He steps into responsibility as it appears... not perfectly, but fully. And in doing so, he changes the timeline. Leadership stops being something deferred... and becomes something lived in real time.

It stayed with me... how much becomes possible when someone decides not to wait to begin.

And it reframes readiness entirely.

Readiness should not be held at a distance... Readiness should not require permission. When someone chooses to begin with what they have, exactly where they are... something powerful unleashes.

What once felt out of reach becomes possible. What once felt distant becomes present. Not because conditions were perfect... but because someone chose not to let the moment pass.

Sometimes the person who changes everything is not the one who waited to be ready.

It is the one who simply began...

Sandra Diaz-Twine

Player • Volunteer • CBS
Survivor Two-Time Winner

2024

"If I tell you I'm coming... I'm coming."

What does it mean to wear a crown... and still choose to walk among the people?

My first LRG happened before I even knew the language for it. There was no framework, no category, no sense of entering a defined community. There was only this quiet certainty... Sandra was going. That alone felt like enough. If Sandra said yes, then something about it had already been tested, already been approved. I followed that instinct, not fully understanding where it would lead, only knowing that something in me was curious enough to find out.

That is how I found myself in North Myrtle Beach, stepping into a *Survivor Celebrity Challenge* that felt both familiar and entirely new. I did not arrive with vocabulary. I arrived with a kind of internal pull, the same one that has always existed around *Survivor*, the one that tightens just slightly in your chest and asks a deeper question... what happens to you when you step inside the game?

What surprised me was not the structure. It was the feeling.

There were no polished sets or invisible production layers holding everything in place. There were folding tables and coolers, handwritten adjustments, players carrying their own belongings from one place to another. There was a sense of something being built in real time, shaped by effort rather than illusion. It could have felt disorganized. It did not. It felt alive.

And in the middle of that movement... there was Sandra.

She was not removed from it. She was not hovering above it. She was moving through it, adjusting something here, asking a question there, reading the space with the kind of awareness that cannot be taught. Her presence was steady and attentive... keenly aware of where things could shift before they actually did. When I asked if she recognized that gift in herself, she answered with the kind of confidence that comes from lived experience.

"Yeah," she said simply. "As a Leo, I'm more of a leader, not a follower."

Meeting Sandra in person does something unexpected. The first thing you notice is not her résumé. It is not the history, the titles, or the legacy that follows her name. It is the way she carries herself in a room that is not asking her to prove anything. There is an openness to her, something grounded and direct.

She told me she lives with an open door kind of approach, something shaped by her time in the Army. "Any body and everybody could come up to me," she said. "Regardless of whatever it was—the conversation that they wanted to have."

That openness is not rooted in obligation. It is rooted in awareness. She understands how easily people can confuse the edited version of a person with the truth of who they are. She has lived long enough with the consequences of that misunderstanding to know that presence can correct it faster than explanation ever could.

At the same time, she does not soften herself into something more palatable. She spoke plainly about her limits. There is intention behind how she shows up. Still, when someone chooses to bring something harsh or unkind into the space, she does not pretend it does not exist.

"I try to be nice to everyone," she told me, "but the minute that can't happen anymore—then, *it is what it is.*" That honesty is not volatility. It is self-awareness. I have *always found straight-shooters* refreshing when so much of the world is coded with nuance and grey matter. Sandra is, without a doubt, a straight-shooter.

As I watched her more closely, what initially looked like helping began to reveal itself as something more layered. She was not simply participating. She was managing. She was reading the flow of the day the way a seasoned leader reads a room, noticing where things slowed, where energy dropped, where decisions needed to be made before the experience began to fray.

She told me she writes notes at night. Not reflective notes, not emotional processing, but precise observations. What needs to shift. What needs to tighten. What must be protected before it unravels.

"This is what you need to change for next year," she said, describing the notes she kept at the end of each day. "I think that comes from the military." Sandra does not simply love the game. She respects what it takes to sustain it.

That respect shows up in unexpected places. She spoke about hosting *Survivor*-style experiences in her own life, turning holidays and gatherings into something immersive and shared. Surviving Christmas. Surviving Thanksgiving. Moments that could be ordinary become something more intentional, something that invites people to lean in and participate rather than simply attend. "Anything I can add *Survivor* to—I do," she told me.

Long before Live Reality Games had a name, she was already part of something similar. She described *Survivor*-style experiences on military bases through MWR* programs, where players traveled and built games for soldiers. That history matters. It reminds us that what we now call a movement did not appear suddenly. It grew slowly, in different places,

---

* Morale, Welfare, and Recreation (MWR) facilities at U.S. military installations provide essential, on-base recreational and support services to boost the quality of life for service members, their families, and retirees.

through people who understood the power of shared experience before there was language to describe it.

When I asked her why she continues to say yes to these opportunities, especially those that exist outside the scale of CBS, her answer was both practical and deeply human. Sometimes it works with her schedule. Sometimes it aligns with travel. Sometimes it connects to something charitable or meaningful.

And then she offered something more... part of it is for her.

She wants time with her people. Not quick interactions. Not moments squeezed between obligations. She wants space. A table. Time to sit, to talk, to exist together without urgency pressing in from every side. "I crave it sometimes," she said. "I can't be on *Survivor* every season—but this is my way of playing."

The *Survivor* community is not simply a network to her. It is something closer to family. Family deserves time and presence. Sandra chooses that space.

◆

When the conversation turned inward, toward what these experiences reveal about her, she did not reach for an idealized answer. She told the truth. She has learned that losing still affects her. It is not about entitlement. It is about care. She described an early experience in an online game where she was voted out first. What stayed with her was not the outcome itself, but the feeling that the elimination carried a certain satisfaction for others.

There is something uniquely vulnerable about being known and then losing in public. It requires a different kind of preparation, one that is not about strategy but about self-awareness.

"I learned that I am a sore loser," she said with complete candor.

She acknowledges that it stings, especially when something matters. That honesty is strength. It is easy to dismiss the pain of losing as trivial. It is not trivial when you are invested. It is not trivial when you care. Sandra does not distance herself from that truth. She holds it.

At the same time, she knows exactly where her deepest loyalty lives.

"My alliance is always going to be to my family, first and foremost," she told me. "There's no confusion about that."

A beautiful clarification about why she plays the way she does, why she separates game from life the way she can, and why her choices carry such fierce internal logic.

♦

When I asked her which Live Reality Game feels closest to *Survivor*, the answer came quickly. *Survival Challenge*. She described it not as a theme, but as an experience. The lack of sleep. The physical demand. The sustained intensity.

"You're sleeping out there for real," she said. "You're going to starve for four days. That one is wholesome—and most like your *Survivor* experience wrapped up into four days."

Her perspective was not dismissive of other games. It was precise. If someone wants to understand what it feels like to be fully immersed, to experience the pressure and endurance that define *Survivor*, that is where they will find it.

Sandra believes these games will continue to grow. Not as a trend, but as something rooted in a deeper human impulse. People are drawn to spaces that allow them to test themselves and experience what version of self shows up when things are uncertain, uncomfortable, and real.

"You really find out what you're all about," she said. "If you want to understand who you are... step into a game." Sandra's crown is not what makes her powerful.

Her willingness to be accessible is.

My Lens Reframed

There are people you expect to feel at a distance. Sandra was not one of them.

Standing with her, I became aware of something I had not fully put into words... how often power creates separation. How it builds space between people over time. And how easily that distance begins to feel necessary... even justified.

She does not lead that way.

She steps into the room... fully present... not above it, but she moves within it. And in doing so, she changes what power feels like. It becomes something you can stand next to. Something you can experience up close.

It stayed with me longer than I expected... that proximity, when chosen intentionally, carries its own kind of authority.

And it reframes leadership entirely.

Power does not have to create distance. There is another way of holding it... one that does not rely on separation to maintain its presence. One that understands that being fully there... visible, accessible, grounded... does not diminish what has been built. It deepens it.

There is awareness required in that. Boundaries that do not close you off... but allow you to remain steady within the space. A kind of endurance that is not always visible... but is felt over time in the way someone continues to show up.

And what stays with me is not only what she has achieved... but how she carries it.

Sandra did not become legendary only because she won.

She became legendary because even with everything she has built... she still walks into the room like she belongs to the people. Crown and all.

Mae Messersmith

Player • Game Production

2024

"I stopped focusing on winning... and started focusing on getting better."

Mae did not enter live reality games chasing a stage.

She entered looking for evidence.

Evidence that she could belong inside a group without shrinking. Evidence that she could contribute without waiting to be invited. Evidence that she could endure uncertainty—physical, social, emotional —and still recognize herself on the other side.

An only child by upbringing, Mae learned independence early. Self-reliance was not a skill she acquired; it was the air she breathed. She learned how to make decisions alone, how to occupy space without depending on others to affirm her presence. What she did not learn as easily was how to trust inside a collective—to believe that her place in a group could be stable, earned, and mutual.

Live Reality Games became a proving ground... not for dominance, but for relationship. Not to conquer others, but to understand herself in motion with them.

She was not trying to be impressive.

She was trying to be sure.

♦

Mae began playing at twenty-five. The early games were harder than she expected—not because of the physical demands, but because of what they stirred emotionally. The woods sang, full with conversation, alliances forming in pockets, names whispered just out of reach. It wasn't hunger that unsettled her. It was ambiguity.

A first boot landed with tremendous weight. Leaving early didn't just feel like losing; it felt like confirmation of a quiet fear she carried with her: maybe I don't register here; maybe I disappear faster than others; maybe my presence isn't missed.

Those early exits lingered longer than they should have. It took time to separate disappointment from identity and outcome from worth. The games ended, but the questions followed her home—into quiet evenings and into reflections she didn't always want to have.

Eventually, Mae did something that required as much courage as entering the game itself: she stepped back. Not away from the community, not away from curiosity, time to come closer to herself.

She shifted into production roles. Production gave Mae distance. Distance gave her clarity.

From the outside, she could see what she had been missing while inside the pressure. She watched how players survived not by brilliance alone, but by contribution. By reliability. By becoming someone others depended on before they were ever feared. She noticed who gathered firewood without being asked. Who steadied conversation. Who made themselves useful before they made themselves strategic.

She learned that the game only overwhelms you when you let it define you.

Mae had been carrying the weight of the outcome too early—win or lose, succeed or fail—when the real work was happening in much smaller, quieter moments.

♦

When Mae returned to playing, she changed her approach. Instead of anchoring herself to a single, crushing objective—win—she worked in increments.

Make it past the first vote.

Be useful at camp.

Hold steady in challenges.

Build one real connection.

Then another.

Progress became cumulative. Confidence became earned.

In her earliest game, Mae didn't gather firewood. She didn't tend the fire. She didn't yet understand that providing for others was not an extra—it was strategy. That lesson arrived quickly. So did others. The scrape of wood against bark. The smell of smoke in her hair. The quiet shift in how people look at you when you become essential.

She learned that consequences are real. That choices echo. That decisions made under pressure don't disappear when the vote is read.

Losses became opportunities to grow. Wins became confirmation. And slowly, almost without realizing it, Mae stopped bracing for failure.

What set Mae apart was not perfection.

It was adaptation.

She learned fast. She adjusted faster. Each experience layered onto the last. And somewhere along the way, people began telling her the same thing. "You would have won."

She dismissed it. Again and again. Until she couldn't.

Surviving Bloomington forced a reckoning. Moments Mae expected to lose, she held. Challenges she doubted, she endured. Decisions she once would have softened, she owned. Mae was playing... as Mae.

A welcome alignment.

For the first time, Mae saw herself the way others had for years—not as potential, but as presence. Not as almost, but as fully capable. The revelation wasn't that she could win. It was that she had never trusted herself enough to believe it mattered.

That realization didn't stay inside the game. It followed her home. It touched how she set expectations. How carefully she protected herself from disappointment. How often she chose safety over conviction.

Live Reality Games allowed Mae to release that habit.

Mae plays now with intention. She values emotional intelligence as much as execution. She understands that how you move through a game shapes how people remember you after it ends. She resists pre-gaming not out of naïveté, but principle—believing the truest test begins when everyone arrives equal, when no one carries advantage except what they build in real time.

Her strength is in her ability to be, see, and trust herself.

My Lens Reframed

There was a lovely moment with Mae where something changed... not in what she did, but in how she began to see herself.

It made me think about how often we move through these spaces bracing for failure... adjusting, protecting, preparing for the moment something confirms the doubt we already carry. And how different everything feels when that pattern loosens... even slightly.

I saw in Mae what happens when someone stops waiting for that confirmation. When they begin to move from a place of self-assuredness.

Mae learned to see herself. Doubt still appears... quickly... ready to define what is possible before anything has even begun. But she does not follow it. She interrupts it.

And over time, something becomes visible.

Confidence is no longer something spoken about.

It becomes something lived.

And what stays with me is this... trusting yourself is not a single decision.

It is something you practice... until it becomes entirely your own.

CHRIS LORD
PLAYER • CREATOR

2025

"This is something we create... and it only exists because people believe in it."

There are creators who chase an idea until it becomes real, and then there are creators who continue showing up long after the idea begins asking something back of them. Chris Lord belongs to the second kind —the kind of creator who understands that what is built eventually begins to require something deeper than vision.

When people talk about *Survivor New York*, they often say his name first. What struck me almost immediately, though, was how quickly Chris redirected the credit. Again and again, he pointed not to himself but to Naomi... her steadiness, her endurance, her devotion. He spoke about her not as support or assistance, but as someone inseparable from the work itself, someone who holds the structure together in ways that cannot be easily seen.

"She really is the heart and soul of the game," Chris told me. "The players usually know of her before they even know about me."

That kind of reverence told me everything I needed to understand. This was not about control. This was about care.

◆

Chris' journey did not begin with a master plan. It began the way so many LRG stories do—by watching from the outside and wanting to step inside. At twenty-three, he flew alone to Arizona to play a live *Survivor*-style game hosted by Chad Liston. He had seen the game on YouTube, tracked it down, and reached out the only way he could.

"I messaged him and said, I want to play this. What do I need to do?" he recalled. "So I'm twenty-three years old. I flew by myself to Arizona."

The setting was stark, the resources minimal, and the heat pressed against the skin in ways that made everything feel more intense. The logistics were held together more by willpower than infrastructure, but the experience moved something in him. He played hard, was voted out, fought his way back, and ultimately won.

"It was a *Redemption Island* theme," he said. "I was voted out and I came back and I ended up winning the game. It was incredible to play both sides of a game like that."

Chris saw the structure, the bones of something larger—a space where strangers became collaborators, where effort turned into meaning, and where people gave themselves fully to an experience that only existed because someone chose to create it.

Soon after, Chris found himself playing *Survival Challenge*, where the scale of production and the level of commitment expanded his understanding of what was possible. The crowds, the coordination, the number of moving parts required to sustain something like that without letting it collapse under its own weight... it revealed a different level of responsibility.

In that space, a realization formed. He did not think about doing it bigger or better. He thought about doing it with intention.

◆

Survivor New York began with the uncertainty many games do— with a *Season Zero* that required asking, inviting, and trusting. Friends and family filled spots, not because they fully understood what they were stepping into, but because they trusted Chris enough to say yes. Sixteen people was the minimum, and sixteen was enough.

From there, it grew.

Each year brought more players, more production, more complexity, and more responsibility. People began traveling across the country, sometimes not even to play, but simply to help. They carried bins, set up challenges, printed materials, and worked through exhaustion because they believed in something that had no network contract and no prize purse—only commitment.

"I have people flying out just to help," Chris said, his voice quieting. "Can you imagine spending your money just to fly out and help for sixteen hours at a game? That gets me emotional that people do that for me." He paused before continuing. "What do they see when I don't believe in myself? What do they see that they believe in this game?"

This is where Chris's story shifts from creation into visionary builder.

◆

At the start of each year, there is nothing. No cast, no logo, no buffs, and no guarantees. There is only the question that waits quietly beneath everything else.

"In January I started with nothing," Chris said. "There's no logo, there's nothing to begin with. There's no players on the roster. I just have to ask myself: Am I ready to take on this challenge again this year? Can I do it? Do I want to do it?"

Chris spoke openly about the cost. The financial strain, the time, the life that is deferred. "I could take that time and I could go on a vacation," he said. "I could take that money, I could do other things. I could visit family."

There is a constant mental tally running in the background while the rest of the world moves toward simpler rhythms.

There have been moments when he has wondered whether the most responsible decision might be to stop. And yet, each year, he returns. Not because the work is easy, but because the community continues to ask for him.

"There's this process where a community has been created and I feel like I'm serving my community," he said. "They're always asking me: what's next? When is *Survivor New York*? I just want to be there."

There is one moment Chris shared that has stayed with me. It was a new location with a tight schedule, and Day One was already behind them. Chris and Naomi walked down a road away from camp, the noise of production fading behind them, both of them overwhelmed.

"We were extremely behind schedule after finishing day one," he said. "Me and Naomi, we looked at each other and I'm like bawling my eyes out. We're walking down the road. I'm like, I don't know how we're going to be able to finish this correctly."

Gravel shifted beneath their feet as they tried to think through what needed to happen next. Both of them were doing the quiet math no one else sees—deciding what could be cut, what had to remain, and what it would mean if the game did not survive the shift.

That was the moment *Survivor New York* stopped being an idea and became a responsibility.

They could have chosen to protect themselves, to pull back or scale down in ways that would have been understandable. Instead, they chose to protect the players. They pivoted, adapted, and finished what they started. It was not perfect, but it was honest, said more than perfection ever could.

"Everything is fixable, everything is interchangeable," Chris said afterward. "When you feel like you're at your lowest, there's only one way to go, and that's up from there. As long as you have somebody that has your back, you're able to work through any tough situation."

Chris said something simply, but it carried enormous weight. "I don't know *Survivor New York* anymore without her." That was not sentiment. It was structure.

Naomi began at the lowest level and rose into a position where she stood beside Chris, not because of a title, but because of trust. Players often knew her name before they knew his. She became a bridge between production and community, between logistics and belonging, between pressure and steadiness.

Chris spoke about her with care, aware of how much she gives and how close burnout can always be. Each season carries an unspoken question about whether she will return, and each time she does, it reinforces the truth that this work is not sustained by recognition, but by belief.

As *Survivor New York* approaches its tenth year, Chris is not focused on endless expansion. He is not chasing visibility for its own sake, and he is not trying to turn the experience into something it was never meant to be.

He is asking what this needs now, what must change in order to stay alive, and what must be released to make space for what comes next. This is not nostalgia. It is discernment, and the difference between the two is what allows something to endure.

When I asked him for a single word to describe his connection to *Survivor New York*, he didn't need to think.

"Creativity," he said.

"These games are going to happen long after we're gone," Chris said. "Fifty years from now, I really think they will still be going on."

He mentioned his two nephews. He hopes they will love *Survivor* the way he does. He imagines one of them taking over *Survivor New York* someday—playing first, then passing it on. "I want to give it to one of them," he said. "I'd love to pass it along and see what happens."

That is not the language of someone holding on. It is the language of someone who understands that the most honest thing a creator can do is prepare their creation to live on without them.

My Lens Reframed

Before sitting with Chris, I thought about creation mostly in terms of vision... the moment something begins... the clarity it takes to bring an idea into form.

What I did not fully understand was what comes after.

There is a different kind of work that follows creation... quieter, less visible... the decision to return. To take responsibility for something that no longer belongs only to you. To keep showing up as it grows, changes, and begins to carry the expectations of others.

With him, I saw what it looks like to stay with something over time... not out of obligation, but because it matters. Creation is not only about beginning. It is about who you are willing to become in order to continue.

And that kind of continuation asks something different.

Not everything we create asks to be admired. Some things ask to be protected... to be carried through uncertainty... through pressure... through the quiet weight of knowing that others have come to depend on what you built.

And over time, something takes form.

It becomes a place people trust... a space they return to... something that holds more than the person who first imagined it.

And what stays with me is this... the things that last are not always the ones that begin the strongest.

They are the ones someone chose to stay with.

Time and time again.

Naomi C.

Player • Volunteer

2026

"I don't have to keep proving I belong."

Naomi does not walk into a room to take it over. She walks in and reads it. There is a quiet attentiveness to her, an awareness that does not demand attention yet shifts it all the same. She notices what is missing before anyone names it. She hears the note that does not quite land. She watches the group the way someone who understands movement watches a stage... who is drifting, who is trying too hard, and who is carrying more than they should, who is about to disappear into the background without anyone noticing.

Then, almost imperceptibly, she begins to adjust.

A chair shifts. A conversation softens. A moment is redirected before it fractures. It is not done for recognition. It is not done for control. It is done because something in her understands how spaces hold people... and how easily they can fail to do so.

That is the kind of leadership that rarely gets noticed or rewarded, but it is also the kind that quietly holds things together.

For a long time, Naomi has been that person. The one who notices. The one who steadies. The one who carries what others do not even realize they have set down. It becomes so natural that it begins to feel less like a role and more like an identity. When you are the person who holds things together, it is easy to believe that everything depends on you continuing to do so.

And eventually, a question begins to surface. Not all at once... not resounding... but persistently.

Is this still bringing me joy... or am I simply being responsible?

There is another question beneath that one, quieter and more revealing. What happens if she steps back from the role she has carried for so long... does everything fall apart, or does she finally get to see who she is without holding everything in place?

That is where Naomi's story lives.

When we spoke, we did not begin at the beginning. There was no need to trace her steps from the outside in. The work we have done together and the conversations shared have already revealed who she is in the spaces she occupies.

"I don't want to be HR anymore," her tone soft, yet decided.

It would be easy to hear that as logistics. It is not. It is emotional labor. It is the role of absorbing tension so others can experience ease. It is managing conflict, holding space, navigating fragile moments, helping people process what it feels like when something that began as fun becomes something more vulnerable.

Being voted out is not neutral. It touches something real. Naomi understands that. She understands what it means to ask people to show up fully... to compete, to connect, to be seen... and then to experience rejection in front of others. That understanding has shaped how she has led, how she has supported, and how she has carried more than most people ever see.

She told me she feels at peace with the idea of not returning to *Survivor New York* in the same way. There was no edge to it. No sense of loss wrapped in defensiveness. It was something steadier... a recognition that something had shifted inside her, and she was willing to honor that shift without forcing herself to remain where she no longer felt aligned.

After the most recent season, she took a trip. Real camping. The kind that strips away convenience and replaces it with something simpler and more honest. The air carried the scent of pine and earth. Smoke clung to her clothes long after the fire had burned down. There was a moment where she caught herself laughing... sleeping outside, immersed in something natural, while also realizing she had been recreating versions of this experience for years.

But the trip was not about the setting.

It was about distance.

In that space, something became clear. She already had what she was once seeking. The friendships. The moments. The people who had quietly become part of her life in ways that did not require constant proximity to be real.

And once you realize that... it becomes harder to continue out of obligation.

She has chosen not to carry it alone anymore. There is strength in knowing when to step back before care turns into exhaustion, before responsibility becomes resentment. That choice is not withdrawal.

It is leadership of a different kind.

Naomi's perspective is shaped by her own experiences of belonging and not belonging. She entered with confidence. She understood the structure. She knew the language. She believed she could navigate it.

"I'm so good," she told me, with the kind of self-awareness that only comes after the fact. "I watch so much *Survivor*. I listen to the podcast. I watch *Australian Survivor*. I understand how to make people like me... and I got voted out second and nobody liked me."

That sentence is its own kind of arrival. Not defeat—revelation.

Instead of closing off, she reflected. She allowed that moment to teach her something about people, about herself, about the difference between understanding a game and understanding connection. That willingness to learn, rather than defend, is what sets Naomi apart.

She did not overreact. She sat with it. And then she went to work on herself—not on her game, but on the parts of herself the game had unearthed. That is a harder kind of practice. It requires willingness to linger inside discomfort rather than move around it.

Naomi laughs when she talks about leadership, as if the word feels too formal for what she has been doing her entire life. The harder lesson has always been trusting that things will continue without her constant presence.

And when she began to step back... she saw that they did.

That realization does not diminish her role.

It frees her from it.

◆

Naomi speaks about the *Survivor* ecosystem with a kind of clarity that only comes from paying close attention. She observes it. She understands how easily something meaningful can become something showy. How quickly proximity can be mistaken for belonging.

"I can give you friendship and you can give me the number of women that I need to play the game," she told me with a laugh that carried both self-recognition and warmth. That recruiter brain never fully powered down.

But what she was giving away was more than logistics. It was herself.

The driving concept behind what she and Chris were building was rooted in something honest and generous.

"99% of us are never going to get on the show," she said. "99% of people have this dream that will not be realized."

That is not a lament. It is the entire point. If the dream cannot be realized on CBS, then you build a place where the dream gets to breathe anyway. Where people who love this thing can live inside it fully, not as a consolation prize, but as something real in its own right.

She is clear about what it cost to hold that vision in place. The emotional weight of it. The invisible labor. The way being the person who cares most can quietly become the person who carries most.

She refuses to let what she loves become something she resents. That refusal is the most generous thing she has done.

♦

When I asked her to describe herself then and now, she did not hesitate. The distance between those two versions of herself contains an entire education.

"Emotional-Loudmouth-*Survivor*-Superfan... annoying," she said of who she used to be, laughing at herself with full affection. "And now I feel like gratitude beyond measure for friends, for friendship, for the hard work and time people give."

The shift is not just internal. It is visible. The energy that once rushed outward, toward the game, toward the structure, toward the next thing—has turned softer. More selective. More honest about what it needs and what it no longer does.

She remembers small moments vividly. An ice cream truck passing through the campground. A pause in the middle of everything to simply exist, to see what they had created—not as a system, but as a collection of people who had found something meaningful together.

Those moments are treasured. They remind her that what she helped built was never just the structure.

It was the connection inside it.

Her relationship with *Survivor New York*, and with Chris, reflects that shift. It is no longer about carrying something alone. It is about trusting what has been built... trusting the people who remain... trusting that the vision does not disappear when she loosens her hold.

Naomi is not running from something.

She is returning to herself.

Listening to her, I found myself wondering how often people confuse usefulness with identity. How often we believe that what we do for others is who we are. How many people do not realize that they are allowed to step away from a role without losing the relationships that were formed within it.

Sometimes the things we love do not disappear. They shift. Sometimes we change before we realize it, and the places that once fit us perfectly begin to feel different—not because they are broken, but because we have grown.

My Lens Reframed

Naomi left me thinking about my time and my passions... and if they were aligned.

There is a moment... quiet, but unmistakable... when something you have carried with care begins to ask something different of you. Not more effort... not more endurance... but honesty.

She did not walk away because it no longer mattered.

She stepped back because it did.

And that stayed with me... the strength it takes to release something you love... before it becomes something you resent.

Naomi also reframed seasons.

Not everything we love is meant to be forever. Some things ask us to stay long enough to give them meaning... and then to listen when they begin to ask for something different in return.

And there is care in that kind of listening.

Change does not erase what was built.

It honors it.

What remains is something lasting... something real... something that does not disappear simply because your role within it has changed. Belonging, then, is not dependent on constant presence. It endures.

And there is a quiet power in choosing differently... not from distance, but from understanding.

Some love stories do not end with one more season.

They end with a quiet, deliberate decision...

I am choosing joy... on purpose.

WORDS OF WISDOM

"As long as you have someone who has your back... you can get through anything."

~ Chris Lord

Trust is built in moments that feel small at the time…
a conversation that lingers a little longer,
a choice that costs more than expected,
a kindness that arrives when it is least deserved.
What begins as proximity becomes connection.
What feels temporary begins to take root.

Part Three
Growth Requires Friction

No space remains comfortable forever. Under pressure, identity sharpens. Bias surfaces. Old wounds speak louder than strategy. The game stops being theoretical and becomes personal. These chapters do not protect the myth of perfection. They tell the truth about what it costs to grow in public. Friction is not the enemy of belonging. It is often the pathway to it — if we are willing to face what it reveals.

"Hunger doesn't create bias. It removes the mask."

~ Renzo Santos

MIRA HALL
PLAYER

2024

"People told me what I couldn't do... and I decided to find out for myself."

What happens when the limits you believed about yourself... quietly fall away... and you realize they were never fixed to begin with?

Mira does not enter the LRG community the way people may expect. There is no polished narrative waiting for her, no lifelong blueprint of strategy or rehearsed certainty about how she will be seen. She does not arrive carrying a version of herself designed for the camera. She arrives the way real people do... through a moment that does not yet feel important enough to name.

A trivia night. A bar humming with laughter and repetition. A conversation that lingers just long enough to capture an unexplained interest. A quiet yes that offers no promises, but a yes that in and of itself holds the possibility of transformation... until it becomes the hinge everything turns on.

Mira's story is not only about games. It is about the quiet, persistent refusal to stay inside the boundaries she was handed—by the world, by her body, by past versions of herself that believed limitation was permanent. It is about what happens when that refusal becomes action... and when action becomes identity.

Long before she ever stepped into a game, Mira had already practiced expansion. She carries a name that was shaped by distance, a version of herself that emerged while she was living in Japan as a teenager. That experience did not simply give her memories. It gave her perspective. It taught her how to exist in unfamiliar spaces, how to move through discomfort without shrinking, how to let the world rearrange her without losing herself in the process.

That kind of experience stays with you. It softens the fear of the unknown. It creates a quiet confidence that says... I have done hard things before. I can do them again.

So when the opportunity came—when a friend introduced her to something strange and slightly unbelievable—she did not need certainty. She only needed curiosity.

When Mira went anyway... something in her felt known.

◆

When I asked her why she plays, she didn't have to ponder.

"I do it to prove to myself that I can go beyond what I think my limits are," she said. "I live and have lived in a plus-sized body my whole life, and I have put a lot of limits on myself because of it—that I thought everyone else was putting on me. I thought I couldn't do the things everyone else could."

Mira has lived in a body that the world often misunderstands. A body that comes with assumptions, spoken and unspoken. Messages about what is possible, what is desirable, what is allowed. Some of those messages were given to her. Some were absorbed slowly. Some became internal truths she carried without questioning.

There was a time when movement itself felt restricted. When the idea of competing in physical challenges felt distant, unrealistic, unattainable. And then she started playing.

The games did not wait for her to feel ready. They asked for her body as it was—in real time, under real conditions. Movement became necessary. Effort became immediate. And with each moment she completed something she once believed she could not do, she experienced a stronger sense of herself.

The story she had once believed began to change.

I am not as limited as I thought.

Mira's realization did not occur overnight. It arrived in layers. Repeating itself until it becomes something she can no longer ignore. Within a year of playing, Mira lost nearly a hundred pounds. Not as a goal, but as a consequence of choosing, again and again, to enter spaces that asked her to move.

And when that shift happens... it does not stay contained to the body.

It expands into identity.

◆

Mira understands that visibility carries pressure. She understands that people are watching, even when she is not performing for them. She knows that her presence alone can challenge assumptions, not through declaration, but through existence.

"I like to think that maybe one or two people—whose friends I played against, who thought they could never do something like this—will watch a game that I've done and be like, wait, she can do that," she said. "Maybe I can do it too."

She is not trying to be a symbol.

And still... she becomes one because she continues to shows up.

There is also a vulnerability in that kind of visibility. Being seen fully, without editing, without protection, without the ability to control how others interpret what they are watching. Mira has experienced that. She has stood in moments of loss that were not private and she has felt the weight of being visible in spaces where emotion cannot be hidden.

That is what outsiders often misunderstand. They reduce the experience to something simple. They see the surface and ask how it could be worth it. They do not understand that what happens inside these spaces cannot be measured from the outside. That connection, intensity, and transformation are not separate from the discomfort—they are shaped by it.

◆

Mira's diagnosis came later, after years of navigating the world without language for what she was experiencing. Autism. ADHD. A framework that allowed her to understand herself without reducing herself to something broken.

In many spaces, she had learned to adjust. To monitor. To edit.

"A lot of the masking that I was taught," she said, "especially as a female, was that I needed to be what appeals to society and be very demure and quiet and don't have a super big personality and don't be crazy... And then you get dropped in the middle of a fake reality world where that's what they want. They want the crazy, outrageous people. They want people who are going to make a splash." She paused. "And I was like, oh—I can just be normal and weird and have my little quirks, and it's perfectly acceptable."

That kind of acceptance is not theoretical.

It is felt.

It allows her to exist fully—not as a version of herself that has been adjusted for comfort, but as the person she already is. And when her body does what her body sometimes does, she names it without ceremony.

"Just so you know," she'll say, if something surfaces, "not freaking out, actually not anxious. My body's just doing things."

A moment for education. Not an apology.

And the response she almost always receives is the same.

Oh, okay. Cool. Fun fact about you.

That is enough. That is more than enough. That is, in fact, everything.

◆

Mira carries a kind of honesty that is both sharp and grounded. She can be direct. She can be playful. She can challenge someone openly and then laugh with them afterward. There is integrity in that—a refusal to separate truth from connection.

She has a line she lives by now. Simple. Declarative.

"Fat is just an adjective," she said. "It doesn't have a negative connotation unless you put one on it."

In a world that has spent decades loading that word with shame, Mira removes the pressure from it. She does not ask anyone else to use it. She does not issue a proclamation. She simply names what is true for her, and in doing so, opens a door for everyone watching who has been carrying that same word differently.

She does not pretend to be easier to understand than she is.

She invites people to meet her where she stands.

That invitation is powerful.

It creates space not only for her, but for others who are watching, wondering if they are allowed to take up space in the same way.

Mira is not asking for that permission.

She is giving it.

When Mira speaks about the future, she holds complexity without trying to simplify it. She wants these spaces to grow—to become more accessible, to reach more people, to remove the financial barriers that keep others from entering. At the same time, she understands the value of intimacy, of connection that does not get lost as something expands.

That tension does not weaken her vision.

It sharpens it.

She is building a life that holds both service and adventure, both grounding and expansion. She works daily with people living with HIV and AIDS, holding space for stories that do not always get to be told in full. She steps into games where her own story gets to unfold in real time.

Through all of it... she remains visible. Not because it is easy.

My Lens Reframed

Being with Mira made me aware of something I had accepted without question.

How easy it is to internalize limits... not because they are true, but because they have been repeated often enough to feel that way. How quickly those stories settle into the body... shaping how we move, where we go, how much space we allow ourselves to take.

She does not move that way.

She moves with a kind of certainty that no longer asks for permission. And in her presence, something begins to loosen. The boundaries that once felt fixed no longer hold.

So much of what Mira shared stayed with me...

How much opens when someone stops organizing their life around what they were told was not possible.

Not all limits are real.

Some are learned... repeated quietly over time until they begin to feel permanent. Until they shape how we move... how we see ourselves... how much space we believe we are allowed to take.

And what I see in her is not resistance... it is decision.

The decision to move fully within the body you have... to trust it... to inhabit it without apology.

That kind of living requires a willingness to act before certainty arrives... to choose differently even when the old narrative still echoes.

And over time, something becomes undeniable.

The room does not shrink.

It makes more space.

When we stop apologizing for taking up space... our lives do not contract.

They expand.

Dejuan Watts

Player

2025

What does it cost to stand firm in your convictions in a game that rewards you for setting them aside?

That question followed me as I listened to Dejuan speak. Everything in the way he tells his story points back to it. Some people talk about these games like they are competition. Some talk about them like they are adventure. Dejuan talks about them like they are *a language*... one that only makes sense if you have lived inside it long enough to understand that the game is never the deepest part.

The depth comes from what is revealed.

He has been living inside that revelation for ten years. Dejuan is not the kind of player who needs to dominate to be felt. He is not interested in spectacle. He is interested in truth. And what makes him different is not that he has figured out how to win the game without feeling... it is that he has never stopped feeling at all.

I asked Dejuan about is recent decision to step away form games for the time being, he spoke about it the way people speak about something they have quietly come to understand. These games require more than time, he explained. They require resources. They require sacrifice. And over time, that accumulation becomes real. Travel. Lodging. Fees. The invisible costs that do not show up until you begin to feel the toll.

But even as he said it, I could feel that money was not the center of his decision. The center was something else entirely.

Dejuan was transparent about what these games ask of you... the part many agree to in theory and struggle to carry in practice. These are games built on deception. We know that. We sign up for that. We tell ourselves that it is contained, that it is temporary, that it is separate from who we are outside of it.

And then it is your hand making the choice. Then it is your voice telling the lie. Then it is someone you care about looking at you as they realize you were not honest with them. And suddenly, it does not feel contained at all.

Dejuan does not run from that tension. He names it. He carries it honestly. He spoke about the discomfort of being good at something that does not align with who he wants to be. About the effects of knowing that you can outmaneuver someone... and still not wanting to be the reason they are hurt.

That is where his integrity lives. Not in avoiding the game... but in refusing to numb himself inside of it.

During the summer of 2025, I witnessed his struggle in real time. A tribal that I have not forgotten. When pressure pushes most people toward actions made from a place of desperation, Dejuan did something different.

He chose clarity over protection.

He told the truth. Dejuan explained that he simply couldn't continue to engage with a player... and continue him to lie. There is something refreshing about that kind of honesty. It does not always make things easier, but it makes them real. And that is who he is.

◆

Dejuan's LRG journey begins the way many of our stories do... with curiosity that turned into action before it fully made sense. He started online, learning the rhythms of the game in a space where everything moves through language and timing. And then he saw something that shifted everything. A game that existed beyond the screen. Real people. Real time. Real challenges.

It sounded unlikely. It sounded impractical. It sounded like something most people would talk themselves out of, but Dejuan decided to play.

He was nineteen. He didn't have extra money and he didn't have a clear path. What he had was determination... and the ability to make a plan work anyway. He moved through obstacles the way he would eventually move through games: with resourcefulness, with a willingness to learn, and one step at a time.

When he arrived, he entered a space where he was immediately aware of something deeper than the game itself. He was the only Black person there. That kind of awareness does not need to be explained. It lives in the body. It sharpens perception. It adds a layer to every interaction. It asks questions that do not always have answers.

That experience did not push him away. It changed him. His first game gave him something he did not expect. Not a title. Not recognition. Something far more lasting. He met his partner there. A relationship that has endured for ten years. A reminder that what we gain from these spaces is not always what we came for... but it is often exactly what we needed.

◆

Over time, he played more. Different formats. Different environments. He knows what aligns with who he is. He is honest about what he enjoys and what he does not. He does not romanticize discomfort for the sake of proving something. He has preferences. And he is clear about them.

What moved him most were spaces where he was not carrying the weight of being the only one. A game designed specifically for Black queer people. A cast where he did not need to translate himself.

"I really wasn't a filler or a placeholder," he told me. "I could be around people that were exactly like me and not feel like a pawn."

Being surrounded by people who reflect your identity does not remove complexity. But it removes the burden of translation. You get to just be.

After years of playing, he reached a moment that many players quietly long for.

A win.

Dejuan followed that with another strong finish. Not by accident. Not by luck alone. By growth. By consistency. By finally allowing himself to see what had always been true.

That he is good at this.

That realization did not come easily. It came after years of questioning. After moments of wondering if he was enough... if he was capable... if he belonged in the way he hoped he did. And when it finally landed, it did not feel like celebration as much as confirmation.

"I always felt like these games, they took a little bit of a hit on your confidence sometimes," he said honestly. "And sometimes I was like, maybe I'm just really not that good. Maybe I can't win."

He had always been that player. He just needed time to believe it.

♦

When I asked him what he values most about these games, he did not talk about strategy. He talked about people. About connection. About the way these experiences open something in us that is difficult to access anywhere else.

"My favorite thing about the games is the people," he told me. "Winning is an added bonus. Of course we all want to win. But I love that I can sit here and have a conversation with you—that's what means the most to me. Because I feel like that is just as great as winning, if not better."

He also spoke about something that deserves more attention than it often receives. The emotional cost of these games... and the lack of systems in place to support it. After ten years of playing, he experienced something new at *Survive*. A space where he could talk. Where he could process. Where he was not required to carry everything alone.

Ten years.

That is both a testament to his resilience... and a reflection of what is missing in the structure of many LRGs.

He spoke about it not with criticism but with gratitude... and with an understanding that if this community is going to continue, it must evolve. It must create structures that care for people not only during the experience... but after it.

The emotional weight does not disappear when the game ends.

As our conversation came to a close, Dejuan shared something that stayed with me long after we stopped recording. He spoke about his mother. About the *Survivor* ritual they shared. Watching together. Talking through the same moments. Living inside that language as something that belonged to them.

"It was our thing," he said. "It was literally our thing that we did together." He lost her when he was seventeen. And he has carried her forward into every space he has entered since.

"I honestly think if she was here, she'd be so proud of me," he said. "Because I think she would be like, you found your community, you found your people. This is what you love and you're good at this stuff." He is certain of it. Not as wishful thinking. As knowing.

There is something powerful about that kind of certainty. About knowing that the life you have built... the people you have found... the way you have chosen to show up... would be seen and understood by the person who mattered most.

My Lens Reframed

With Dejuan, I became aware of something I had not fully put into words.

How often these spaces reward distance... the ability to detach, to separate feeling from action, to move through the game without letting it touch you too deeply.

He does not move that way.

He stays present... fully aware of what he is feeling, without letting it pull him off center. And in doing so, he reshapes what strength looks like. It is no longer about control through detachment... but about remaining grounded, even while everything around you is shifting.

Dejuan's tenderness toward others stayed with me... the discipline it takes to feel fully... and still be yourself.

There is more than one way to move through games.

To stay fully engaged... to feel what is happening as it unfolds... and still hold onto who you are requires something deeper. Intention. Trust.

A willingness to believe that staying real will not cost you everything... especially not the parts of yourself that matter most.

You do not have to lose yourself to belong.

You do not have to harden to compete.

There is another way.

And what's left is this... being fully yourself... even in a game... may be the most powerful strategy of all.

DANIEL SUCKOW

PLAYER

2026

"I need to prove to myself that I'm not the same person."

I was not there, but I should have been.

My absence stayed with me in a way I did not expect. I was supposed to be there. There was a camera in the woods that belonged to our documentary, someone I trusted moving through the same space I should have been walking. I remember where I was when the message reached me, and I remember the word that arrived without context, without explanation, without anything to steady it.

A *knife*.

Fear rose before understanding had the chance to catch up. My thoughts went immediately to my videographer and friend, to the responsibility I carry for the people I have asked to step into these spaces with me. There was a sharp awareness that I could not protect my crew, could not slow anything down, could not offer presence in a moment that might have needed it. Anger followed close behind, not only at what may have happened, but at the realization that something had unfolded in a space I care deeply about that lacked the intentional structure the moment called for.

By the time I spoke to Daniel, I understood how quickly a story can begin to take shape without the full picture.

Daniel did not reach out to defend himself. He posted a question about the documentary. He wondered how he would be portrayed. There was no attempt to control the narrative, no urgency to correct or persuade. What I heard instead was concern about what would linger after the moment had passed.

Before we moved into what happened, I wanted to understand who he is when he is not inside a game. I wanted to understand the person.

I learned that Daniel is someone who is building toward a life of teaching. He spoke about students with a genuine interest in how people learn, how they struggle, how they are shaped by the environments they are placed in. He is thoughtful in a way that takes a moment to notice. He does not rush his words. He considers them. There is a quietness to him that could easily be overlooked in boisterous spaces.

"I don't see myself as an aggressive person," he told me. "I'm usually the one trying to keep things calm."

That context does not erase what happened. It deepens it.

He had driven hours to be there, the kind of drive that stretches anticipation across long miles. He spent money and time in ways that reflect commitment more than convenience. He came for what so many come for... connection, challenge, the possibility of belonging inside something immersive and shared.

When he described the challenge just before his elimination, his language shifted slightly, the pace of his words tightening as he moved back into the moment. He had been placed in a high pressure role, the kind where attention narrows and expectation sharpens. Immediately after, he was pulled into interviews. He described no pause between intensity and reflection, no space for his body to settle or for his thoughts to organize. He did not return to his tribe and within minutes, he was voted out.

"I didn't even get a second to breathe," he told me. "It was just… from one thing straight into the next."

While the order of events held a familiarity for me, I could see there was a disorientation that came with that sequence for Daniel. The body still carrying intensity when it is suddenly asked to absorb loss. Emotion can rise faster than language can meet it.

He walked away. He raised his voice once into open space, then chose distance.

When he returned, the atmosphere had shifted. He described it as quieter, but not calm, as if something had settled between people that no one was naming. He felt outside of it, without direction, without a clear understanding of what came next.

◆

That is where the moment with the knife enters the story, and it is more complicated than the word itself allows.

Daniel had a pocketknife. He explained that he often carries one. He began opening and closing it, a small, repetitive motion, something to do with his hands when his energy had nowhere to go.

"I was just flicking it," he said. "Like a fidget. I wasn't thinking about how it looked. I was just trying to calm down."

In his body, it was regulation. In the space around him, it was something else. "I never meant to scare anyone," he said. "That wasn't where I was at all."

Both of those things can be true at the same time. A person can be managing their internal state while someone else is experiencing that same behavior as a potential threat. The distance between those two experiences can close quickly, especially in an environment already shaped by stress, fatigue, and heightened awareness.

What we call a game is, in practice, an environment of layered pressure. There is limited food, heat that presses against patience, exhaustion that lowers the space between thought and reaction, and social dynamics that shift rapidly. When a player is removed from that environment suddenly, the body does not reset at the same speed.

Daniel described sitting inside that drop, the sudden absence of purpose, the energy still moving through him without a place to land. There was no structured support, no clear transition, no shared process for what happens to a player in that space between participation and departure.

♦

Creators committed to player safety, must respond when fear enters the space.

Daniel was asked to leave. Night had already settled in. He described trying to sleep, but not fully resting. The following morning stretched into waiting without clarity, without conversation, without a shared understanding of what had occurred.

"It felt like I didn't get a chance to explain anything," he said. "Like the decision had already been made."

Later, after posting a *Youtube* video about his game experience, Daniel had been removed from casting spaces. There was no structured conversation, no opportunity to process the moment in a way that allowed for accountability and understanding to exist together.

This is where the questions move beyond a single person... conversations the community must have.

What does safely look like?

Who defines that standard?

What behaviors cross a line?

Who is blacklisted and why?

Is there an appeal process or an opportunity to be heard?

These questions are not theoretical. They are already shaping outcomes.

Daniel did not ask me to excuse what happened. When I asked him what he would say now, he answered without hesitation. "I should have put it (the knife) away," he said. "I can see how that looked. I just wish I had been able to say that then."

There is a difference between denial and reflection. He was not trying to erase the moment. He was trying to understand it... and to be understood within it.

Our conversation did not lead to a clean conclusion. It is the tension between protection and possibility. It is the question of whether a person can make a mistake inside a high pressure environment and still be given a path forward. It is the question of who decides when that path is closed, and what process exists before that decision becomes final.

I return to the moment I heard that single word and felt my own reaction rise ahead of understanding. That awareness does not soften the seriousness of what unfolded. It sharpens my sense of responsibility.

If a moment can be defined that quickly from a distance, then what we build inside these spaces matters even more.

Not only in how we prevent harm, but in how we respond when something human and imperfect unfolds in front of us.

MY LENS REFRAMED

This chapter did not leave me with answers. It left me with responsibility... and the recognition that there are conversations we avoid... until we can't.

I found myself thinking less about the moment itself and more about what surrounds a moment like this... the structures we build, or fail to build, to hold people when something fractures. These spaces are not just containers for strategy. They hold emotion... identity... stress... histories we do not always see.

They hold humans.

When those elements collide... the outcome is not always clean.

What stays with me is how quickly perception can take over when process is absent. It fills the silence. It shapes the narrative. It decides, often too quickly, who someone is allowed to be next.

Not every moment resolves cleanly. Some reveal what was never fully built to hold it. They draw attention beyond the event itself... to the structure around it... to what was prepared... and what was not.

There is responsibility in that.

Not only to protect... but to respond with care. To recognize that intent and impact do not always align... and that both require attention. That accountability and humanity are not opposites... even when they are hardest to hold together.

What happens in those moments does not only shape what is remembered...

It can shape who someone is allowed to become next.

Jaymes Lanoye

Player

2026

"I had to learn how to stand and clap for myself when there was no one there to do it."

I noticed Jaymes before I knew his story.

He was sitting with someone else's pain as if it belonged in his hands. A tribe-mate had just been voted out of a game—a brutal ending, complicated emotions, the kind of moment that lands differently when you are already carrying something. Jaymes saw more than the surface of it. He sensed the kind of grief that makes the air feel heavier, the kind that makes even laughter feel out of place. He did not rush to fill the silence or offer a false sense of comfort. He did not try to fix what could not be fixed.

He simply sat down, took the man's hands, and stayed.

Later, he told me he could feel it... pain so sharp it began to ignite inside his own body, as if empathy itself was fire.

I noted this early about Jaymes... even when he is exhausted, even when his own history would justify distance or bitterness, he continues to reach toward people with warmth. And warmth is not something he was always given.

What does it mean to survive your childhood and then enter a game that strips you bare... calling back some of your childhood pain?

Jaymes came to me differently than most contributors in this project. He did not wait to be invited. After reading Dejuan's chapter, he reached out and said, "I have a story too." There was no performance in it, no attempt to impress. It felt like something simple and honest... an ache that had finally found words.

So I told him we would talk.

When the interview began, I noticed his shirt before anything else. Black with white letters across the front that read: *Be Kind*. It didn't feel like fashion. It felt like a decision he was still making every day.

Within minutes, he began to cry. Not in a way that asked for attention or softened the moment, but in a way that felt real and unguarded. The kind of tears that arrive without permission. He warned me there would be more.

I told him that was good. Pain and shared tears are difficult for me. I was raised not to cry and sadly spent the great part of my life holding my breath... and my tears. I now understand how flawed that teaching was and I work very hard to allow space for whatever is needed. Tears are real. Necessary. *Human.*

"I've been on my own since I was 15," Jaymes began. "I hopped couches of friends and there was a period of homelessness. I am the child of two drug addicts. My father was the president of a motorcycle gang. And I had to teach myself a lot of things. A bag of failures turned into triumphs is basically how I feel."

He paused thoughtfully, "I'm just somebody that didn't give up and somebody that just chose to take a different path."

Jaymes learned to read people early. He watched faces, tracked tone, noticed hands, and felt shifts in energy before they were spoken aloud. Awareness was not optional for him. It was how he stayed safe.

And still, even in that chaos, he found moments that told him he mattered.

At thirteen, he was recognized as one of five youth leaders in his city.

The ceremony should have been a celebration. Instead, it became a moment of contrast. Other children were surrounded by families, cameras, and applause. Jaymes sat alone. The kind of alone that expands inside your chest and presses against your ribs. Someone commented on it—not cruelly, but enough for it to land.

He refused to let that become the story that defined him. Instead, he turned it into something else. He told himself he was special. That he was doing this on his own... *that he was going to make it out.*

Even earlier, at eight years old, he had been placed in a gifted program. Both parents attended the meeting—which should have felt like safety, but his father appeared irritated to be there. Jaymes absorbed what children absorb quickly: that his excellence was inconvenient and that his brightness took up too much space.

Years later, in therapy, he would come to understand something a child cannot yet process. People can only meet you where they are. His father was not equipped to love in ways that felt like love. That is not a child's failure, but children do not translate that way. And sometimes, the takeaway is that they must work to become worthy.

◆

At fifteen, Jaymes would try out for varsity volleyball... he did not make the team. The coach told him to lose some weight and return the following year. For some, that moment would have become a reason to stop. For Jaymes, it became a beginning.

He lost eighty pounds. He came back. He made the team. He even started. Jaymes was named *Most Improved* at the season-end banquet. The very coach who had once dismissed him gave a heart-felt and moving speech before presenting Jaymes with the *Unsung Hero Award.*

Jaymes has developed the ability to transform rejection rather than internalize it. He shared that when he later made the varsity team, he would go to that same coach during practice and say, "Just tell me what I need to work on. Tell me what I'm not doing. I don't want the compliments. I know the good that I'm doing, but I really want to be a good part of this team."

That instinct—toward honest feedback, toward growth over

comfort—has followed him everywhere. He walks into new jobs and tells managers the same thing. He enters games with the same orientation. He wants to know what he is missing so he can close the gap.

A phrase he loves and lives by is *alive out of spite.* There is laughter in it when Jaymes shares... and also truth. The spite is not about bitterness. It is about the refusal to disappear simply because disappearing would have been easier.

◆

Somewhere along the way, Jaymes made himself a promise. "The biggest mantra of my life," he said, "is be who you needed when you were younger."

For a long time, that promise led him to people pleasing. He gave too much. He stayed too long. He made himself smaller so others could be comfortable. He became the *doormat-friend*, the one just trying to keep people in his life.

Eventually, he learned something different. He learned to set boundaries. He learned that he could remain soft without disappearing. He learned that advocating for himself did not require giving up the kindness he had worked so hard to choose.

He described never wanting his pain to harden him. He had seen where that road leads and vowed to never hate being alive. "It feels so much better to empower and uplift," he said quietly. "I could absolutely be an asshole seven days a week. But it's more fulfilling—your cup is filled up more—just by being kind."

There were people along the way who changed his life. Cathy, his father's partner, is one of them. He carries her name on his wrist. He describes her as *one of the greatest people he has ever known*, someone who likely saved his life.

She died when he was nine.

His relationship with his father was marked by abuse. He remembers not being allowed to use the computer to complete a school assignment, so Jaymes went to the library. When he returned, his father hit him and pushed him down a flight of stairs.

Jaymes got on his bike and rode to the *YMCA*, where he was part of a youth leadership group. He walked in and asked for help.

They gave it to him.

He spent time in transitional housing before he moved back in with his mother— in a condemned building without heat or reliable water. He learned to boil water for bathing and he learned to live with instability... and he learned to love someone who was still struggling.

At fifteen, he received a call that his mother had been severely attacked. He reacted with anger and fear, grabbing a bat and going looking for the man responsible. He reflects on that moment now as one that could have ended everything.

Jaymes couldn't find the man. If he had, Jaymes may not be here now.

As he grew older, he began to understand his mother's life more fully. Her childhood trauma. Her pain. Her addiction. The ways she coped... and he chose to forgive her. They rebuilt their relationship. She told him, near the end, that he was the greatest thing she had ever done.

That sits with him. He carries it.

◆

In 2022, she almost died. He flew to her, stayed by her bedside, authorized procedures, held her hand, and watched her recover. She began documenting her medications, writing letters, healing parts of herself that had been broken for decades.

That was the season of life he was in when he played *Survive* in 2023. A week before the game began, his father entered hospice.

The next day, he died.

Jaymes did not know how to hold it. He felt guilt for not feeling what he thought he should. He felt grief in his body even when his mind could not fully embrace it. He considered withdrawing and cancelling his plans to travel to McHenry, Illinois.

He did not.

"The reason I want to be on *Survivor*," he said, "is because I've literally been surviving since I was four."

Jaymes has played sixteen LRGs across nine years. He can walk into a room and instantly read it. He can feel the micro-shifts in energy before they are expressed. He can tell when someone is about to turn on him before they have made the decision themselves. He knows exactly where that gift comes from.

It comes from trauma. He knows that.

When he handed over his phone at the start of *Survive,* he sat down at the bar outside, put on his sunglasses, and collapsed. He spent the first hours of the game breaking privately, walking away to cry somewhere production could see him but no one else could. The production team knew what he was carrying. He recalls how gentle the team was with him such that their care is felt in his retelling.

At last, during a tribal council, he could no longer contain his emotions. His tribe asked about his tears. He told them his father had died a week earlier. He had been hiding it because he did not want it to become a storyline or a sympathy vote.

His tribe cried with him. One player removed a peace-signed necklace from her own neck and placed it in his hands... which now hangs on his mother's urn.

Jaymes continued to play. He pushed through physical pain and emotional weight. He won the final immunity and remembers asking to call his mother on her birthday and offered to take a penalty for it. Production said yes. He called her, cried openly, told her he loved her, and then went back to the game.

He describes the jury with precision. No time to process. No separation from the experience. Emotions without space to settle. He felt attacked in ways that went beyond gameplay. Comparisons were made to some of the most notorious villains in *Survivor* history.

Jaymes left before the votes were read. He needed distance.

A week and a half after the game ended, his mother died... leaving the game and his grief permanently intertwined.

After her death, Jaymes stepped away from LRGs. He entered therapy and began to untangle what he had relied on to survive—the hyper-vigilance, the caretaking, the way he had learned to make himself useful to ensure he was kept. He learned that strength did not have to mean constant vigilance. He learned that being the person others needed did not require erasing himself.

"There's so many other blessings on the other side of pain," he told me. "There's so many reasons to get up and start the day. And for the longest time, I would sleep eight, ten, twelve hours because I was very, very depressed. And now when I go to sleep, it's hard to turn my brain off because I just want to wake up and have it be tomorrow."

When Jaymes finally returned to LRGs, he remembers one in particular when butterflies appeared across the field. They were everywhere... his mother loved butterflies. And he knew...

He carries part of her everywhere now—a travel urn, "...because she never got to see the world," he said. "Where I go, she goes."

◆

Live Reality Games gave Jaymes something real. Not symbolic—real. He built a life with people he met through these experiences. He now lives in a four-bedroom house with three people he met through games. He has a community that calls him when it matters and shows up when it counts.

When I asked him why the games mattered even after everything he had been through, he explained his emotion and tears when his games comes to an end: "I'm not crying because I'm getting voted out. *I'm crying because I'm leaving the bubble.* I'm mourning that already. And getting voted out isn't so much about the pain that my game is ending. It's about the fact that this experience is ending. And this experience has been beautiful."

He calls it a hidden beauty. When you are in the game, with no phone, sitting around a fire, laughing with people who showed up fully... it feels like the Thanksgiving dinner table he never had. It feels like belonging that does not require explanation.

◆

Jaymes has a vision for what comes next. He believes he will reach

Survivor. He wants to write his autobiography—*In My Boots*, named after his original last name. He wants to speak. To teach. To stand in front of rooms full of young people who are sitting where he once sat, and to tell them something he had to discover the hard way.

"You are the CEO of your life," he would tell them. "All the choices that you make are going to have good and bad consequences. And when you fail, it's just an opportunity to fall apart and rebuild yourself better in the image of who you want to be."

He also believes in accountability. He told me plainly that he will call out anyone—even his closest friends—when something is wrong. "It costs zero dollars and zero cents to be a good person," he said. "And not everybody is good. Silence is complicit."

As soft as he is, he stands firm. Both things are true at the same time and he has learned how to hold them.

What you are not changing, you are choosing... that is another of his mantras.

He means it as a call to action, not condemnation. He applies it to himself first. He keeps going back to therapy. He keeps naming what he is working on and he keeps striving toward who he wants to be.

MY LENS REFRAMED

Jaymes is no longer the child sitting alone at a ceremony.

He is the embodiment of kindness... surrounded by butterflies... sitting in quiet presence as he holds another's hand in a moment of grief. And in that image, something settles. He has become the person he needed when he was a child.

There is a depth to that kind of becoming... a willingness to carry what was once painful without allowing it to harden into something that closes you off from the world. To move forward with awareness of what you have lived through... and still choose something softer... something more connected.

It is not automatic. It is a choice. A decision made again and again... to be open... to stay present... to extend care even when it would be easier to withdraw.

And there is something profoundly powerful in that. Not in the absence of pain... but in the way it is carried.

Because what he offers now... is what he once needed most.

Renzo Santos

Player

2026

I noticed Renzo before he spoke. He carried a quiet presence that was not withdrawn or hesitant, but observant and grounded. He smiled easily and generously, offering warmth without effort, and yet there was something deeper beneath that lightness. When I looked more closely, I saw it in his eyes... alert, measuring, aware. Stillness is often misread, but with Renzo it was not absence. It was attention.

He moved through the game like someone who had learned long ago that watching can be safer than acting too soon. His silence was not uncertainty. It was calibration. You could feel him tracking the room, sensing energy, and holding space without needing to control it. There was a quiet current to Renzo, something constant and grounded just beneath the more visible waves.

◆

Renzo was born and raised in the Philippines in a conservative family, in a culture where queerness rarely came with language, and even less often with affirmation. There were no visible models for how to be both gay and whole at the same time. There was no roadmap for masculinity that could hold gentleness and strength together without contradiction. In that absence, he learned to adapt, to excel, and to make himself undeniable.

"Microsoft Excel was my first love," he laughed, with the kind of smile that is both self-aware and completely serious. "I often tell people that."

He became fluent in systems, drawn to numbers, finance, and structure. Spreadsheets offered something the world did not always provide. Cells aligned. Columns balanced. Equations resolved. In a life that could feel undefined, numbers followed rules. They created a sense of order that he could rely on.

Immigrating to the United States on a scholarship was not only an act of ambition. It was an act of risk, shaped by pressure as much as opportunity. San Francisco did not happen by chance. His life there was constructed carefully, built line by line, with intention behind every step. By the time Renzo entered the Live Reality Games community, he had already lived multiple lives. He had been an immigrant, a finance professional, a DEI advocate, a podcast producer, and a gay man who had learned how to succeed without ever fully resting.

He told me something that I want to offer here, because it speaks to the world he navigated before any game ever began.

"I really think the world is not a zero sum game," he said. "We can always uplift each other."

He carries that belief the way some people carry a compass. It does not make every step easy. But it keeps the direction clear.

◆

Survivor mattered to him long before Live Reality Games did. As a young man watching *Survivor*, something shifted when he saw Charlie, one of the first openly gay players portrayed not as a caricature but as complex and strategic. That moment mattered more than it may have seemed. For the first time, queerness was not reduced or simplified. It was not presented as a punchline or a limitation. It was shown as power.

He did not yet know how deeply that image would stay with him.

Like others, Renzo's path into LRGs began during COVID, when isolation created the space for discovery. He found online games, then a community, then something called *Sequester*, and then the realization that live games existed at all... but Renzo had conditions for how he would enter and what games he would play.

"I'm only going to play a game where I have to sleep in a jungle or forest or wilderness," he told me. "I'm a big city boy growing up. So this is all out of my comfort zone. I will only do that if I would represent a charity."

He played *Live to Give* with a broken wrist. He did not scale back. He competed fully. He told me about the first physical challenge at *Survive*, about facing someone taller, seemingly stronger, and discovering that he was the one who held on longer.

"How poetic it is," he said quietly, "that I'm using my wrist for that specific challenge, which I broke—and which was a trigger for a lot of the self-healing that I had to do."

◆

When Renzo stepped into *Survive* in the summer of 2025, he did not arrive chasing dominance. He came with curiosity, with openness, and with a genuine interest in what games designed with intention might reveal about people under pressure. From the beginning, he moved differently. He listened more than he spoke. He built relationships. Genuinely. He tracked subtle shifts in tone the way he once tracked market fluctuations, noticing patterns that others overlooked.

There was another Asian man in the game. They did not seek each other out deliberately. There was no whispered agreement or strategic alignment. There was simply a familiarity that required no explanation. Two men carrying layered histories into the same compressed space, sharing a presence that felt recognizable even without words.

That proximity became enough.

In games shaped by scarcity, familiarity can quickly turn into narrative. Two becomes a pair, and a pair becomes a threat. Hunger does not create bias. It reveals it. Sleep deprivation narrows the space between instinct and reflection, and under pressure, the mind looks for patterns it can categorize quickly.

Difference becomes something that can be sorted.

Renzo felt the shift before it was spoken. He had lived it before, in rooms where sameness meant safety and difference carried consequence.

"I was celebrating internally that there were two Asian men," he said. "Kudos to the production team for being able to make it happen. But that was weaponized against me."

He recognized the feeling of being measured not as an individual, but as part of a category that others could define more easily than they could understand. There was no overt malice, and there did not need to be. What stayed with him was not simply that he became a target. It was how quickly the logic of that targeting made sense to others.

"When we're deprived of sleep, when we're deprived of food," he said, "all the filters go away. And all the uncomfortable, but very needed, conversations do happen."

◆

There came a moment, quiet and unremarkable on the surface, when Renzo understood what the game was asking of him. He could separate himself. He could vote against the person who reflected parts of his own identity. He could align with the narrative and call it strategy. It would have been easy to justify.

Instead, he paused.

"If you're making me vote for the other Asian man," he said, "I'll be invalidating everything that I stand up for. So I will not vote for him."

He did not accuse or confront. He did not turn the moment into a speech. He simply chose not to survive by erasing himself.

That choice did not appear heroic in the moment. It appeared costly, and it was. His torch was snuffed earlier than he had hoped. The flame faded, the smoke lingered, and he walked away not in anger, but in thoughtfulness. He was not broken by the experience, but he was unsettled by what it revealed.

The months that followed were quieter than the game itself. There were affirmations from production and from fellow players, but there were also losses. There was the story he did not get to finish, the arc that never fully unfolded, and the familiar ache of being misunderstood in spaces that promise fairness but do not always deliver it.

When we spoke, Renzo was not raw. He was integrated.

He spoke with a calm clarity, without defensiveness or sharpness. There was no need to prove anything. There was only reflection that had settled into understanding.

◆

He told me something simple, something that carried the weight of conclusion rather than aspiration.

"I am enough," he said.

For much of his life, success had been measured through accumulation. Degrees, promotions, recognition, and external validation shaped the way he understood progress. *Survive* disrupted that equation. It replaced it with a quieter question. Who are you when advancement is no longer the measure?

"Being able to reimagine my concept of success," he said, "was something that I can tangibly take away from playing these live reality games."

Renzo no longer defines survival by how long he lasts. He defines it by alignment. It is the ability to be himself under pressure, to choose integrity even when it comes at a cost, and to allow a moment to take something from him without allowing it to take who he is.

That understanding did not belong to the woods. It followed him into his work, into relationships, and into leadership spaces where subtle bias continues to exist beneath polished language. He softened where he had once protected himself too tightly. He strengthened where he had once overextended himself.

The game did not break him. It clarified him.

When I think about Renzo now, I do not think about the vote. I think about coherence. I think about a man who refused to fracture himself for the sake of advantage. I think about someone who understands that while hunger can strip away comfort, it cannot define identity unless you allow it to.

MY LENS REFRAMED

Renzo called me to pay attention to moments I might have missed before.

Not the visible ones... not the moves that draw attention... but the quieter decisions. The ones made internally... where something is weighed, considered, and chosen without anyone else fully seeing it happen.

He brought into focus how much of these games live there.

The rules are not always neutral. The conditions are not always fair. And still... within that... there is choice. Not always about what happens... but about who you are willing to be as it unfolds.

Not every decision is visible.

Some of the most important ones happen quietly... in the space between what is possible and what feels right.

And what I witnessed in Renzo is a willingness to hold that line. To recognize when a path forward asks for something that does not belong to you... and to choose differently... even when it costs you.

That is courage. Not staying in the game... but staying with yourself... even under pressure. Refusing to trade alignment for advancement... refusing to move in a way that separates you from who you know yourself to be.

Renzo did not leave the game unfinished.
He left it intact.
And left is an understanding that shifts everything...
Walking away as yourself... is not a loss.
It is the truest form of survival.

KADIE YANNONE

PLAYER • REALITY RETREAT OWNER

2026

"I get to be me."

Kadie did not start in the woods. Her story began in a hospital, in a moment that did not resemble the soft, cinematic version of motherhood people often imagine. At thirty-three weeks pregnant, swollen and uneasy, she went to what she assumed would be a routine appointment. Instead, she was admitted. A week later, after two days of labor, she underwent an emergency C-section, and her son was taken immediately to the NICU.

She was told she could see him the next day.

She refused to wait.

They wheeled her upstairs that night, and she met Quinn. That beginning matters because it stripped away any illusion that motherhood would be gentle. It taught her immediately that love and fear can exist in the same breath. Before that moment, she had never worried much about her health, but once you hold a child whose survival feels connected to your own, something shifts. Vigilance becomes constant. A quiet hum of responsibility settles into the background, and the nervous system no longer fully powers down.

Eighteen months later, the world shut down. The pandemic collapsed whatever village she might have leaned on, and the house seemed to grow smaller as the responsibilities grew larger.

During that time, she read about flamingos. Flamingos are pink because of what they consume, but after they give birth, they transfer nutrients to their offspring and their color fades. Some turn nearly white, and it can take years for them to regain their pink. The blog called it getting your pink back.

For Kadie, that idea was revelation. She realized she did not need to be vibrant and fully expressed in every season. She could be white for a while. She was giving everything to her child, and that understanding allowed her to offer herself grace.

Grace does not erase longing. Beneath that acceptance was a quiet awareness that she missed parts of herself. The parts that existed outside of diapers, nap schedules, and the constant mental tracking of everything that needed to be done.

When Kadie was invited into live reality games, her first fear was not hunger or competition. It was leaving Quinn. She had never been away from him for more than twenty-four hours, not in a way where she could still check in or receive updates.

A week before her first game, she asked her husband the kind of question that carries more vulnerability than any strategic move ever could. "If I quit," she asked him, "will you still love me?"

This was not a question about failure. It was a question about worth. About whether she would still be enough if she could not carry everything at once.

Together, they created a signal. If she needed reassurance during the game, she would look at him, and he would mouth two simple words. Quinn's good. It was a small thing. It was enough.

Then she stepped into the woods, and something unexpected

happened. Relief. "I don't even have to shower," she told me, laughing. "I don't even have to eat. I don't have to make a meal. All I have to do is survive a vote. And I was like—moms can do hard things."

It was not that she loved her child any less. It was that for the first time in years, she was not responsible for meeting anyone else's needs. There were no meals to plan, no schedules to manage, and no invisible labor quietly running in the background. She was in the woods, and the only responsibility was survival.

In that space, she realized something that felt almost surprising in its honesty. Compared to motherhood, this felt manageable.

◆

Kadie studied both theater and psychology. When she describes the combination, she does not treat it as unusual. To her, it makes complete sense. Theater taught her to recognize performance, while psychology helped her understand what exists beneath it.

As a therapist, she believes that behavior is rarely about a single moment. It is shaped by everything that came before. All the yesterdays, she calls them. That instinct follows her into the game.

"I understand that everyone has needs," she said. "And if I can shape myself into an answer for someone's need, then they'll want me in their alliance."

She does not say this with coldness. She says it with the ease of someone for whom people have always been the study and the joy. Understanding is not manipulation for her. It is care with strategy inside it.

In her first live game, she played with heart. She chose to open a discovered box rather than hide it. Inside were small comforts, food and items that could ease the experience for the group. She believed integrity would matter.

She was voted out first.

The pain lingered longer than she expected, not because she lost, but because it challenged her understanding of what it meant to do the right thing. She realized that her internal definition of fairness was not shared by everyone else. In later games, she did not abandon her heart. She added clarity. She stopped assuming others understood her intentions and began communicating more directly.

Her growth was not about becoming hardened. It was about becoming more complete.

♦

There is a moment from one of Kadie's later games that tells you everything you need to know about who she is when the pressure becomes most real.

She was at the Final Four. She had built a genuine friendship with a player named Jesse, the kind of friendship that forms in the dark, in the exhausted hours between tribal councils, when someone tells you something true about their life and you tell them something true about yours. She had told Jesse she would not write his name down. She meant it.

The math of the game offered her a path to the end. She could use it. Jesse's torch would go out, and she would have a better shot at winning.

She did not take it. "I don't need that win," she told me simply. "I need that relationship."

She lost that game on a puzzle. The person she had aligned with throughout won. Kadie does not carry regret about that choice. She carries Jesse. A text here, a message there, months apart and still real. A moment in time that belongs to them, and that no outcome can reach back and erase.

She is clear about the distinction: if there had been a million dollars on the line, the math might have looked different. But in a game built on community, where the win matters but the people matter more... she chose the people.

♦

Kadie and her husband, Allen, made a decision that reveals something essential about how they approach their life together. At the start of the pandemic, they chose to begin couples therapy. Not because anything was broken. Because they did not want anything to break.

"We went to couples therapy," she told me, "not because we were having problems, but because we wanted to prepare to never have problems."

That sentence alone is something I want to put on a wall. Every Wednesday, they have a ritual. Sushi. Therapy. *Survivor.* In that order. It is deliberate, protected, and non-negotiable. I believe her when she says it is her favorite night of the week.

That partnership is what allows her to step into the woods without guilt consuming her. She knows Quinn is good. She knows Allen has it. She knows she can return and nothing essential will have frayed.

Her vision for what comes next is both clear and expansive. She wants to raise sons who understand the strength of women. Not because they were told. Because they saw it, lived alongside it, and carried it into the world with them.

She is also building the *Reality Retreat* alongside Allen and Brandon Clark, a permanent space where Live Reality Games, community, and connection can happen with intention. She describes it with the energy of someone who cannot sleep because her mind is too full of possibility.

"So much of our world is pathologized," she said, "when all someone really needs is connection. What if we could treat people by just a competitive, fun experience in the woods?"

She sees the retreat as more than an LRG venue. She sees it as a place where people who do not fit neatly into categories can arrive and find their people. Where kids who are the only gay person in their class or the only one watching *Survivor* by themselves in their town can step into a space and exhale.

She is building it because she knows what it means to step into a place where you finally feel like yourself.

MY LENS REFRAMED

Motherhood is often described as sacrifice, but what I saw in Kadie was something more layered.

I saw a woman allowing herself to recognize her multi-faceted and complex nature, even within the demands of being needed. She did not disappear into motherhood. Parts of her paused... not erased, not lost... just quieted for a season. And when the time was right, she stepped forward again. Not as someone new... but as someone returning to herself.

That distinction stayed with me.

Her time in the woods was not about leaving her family. It was about remembering who she is beyond being needed... and recognizing that healing does not always look like rest. Sometimes it looks like choosing yourself intentionally... even in small, quiet ways.

There are seasons where we give more than we receive. Where parts of ourselves soften or go quiet... not because they are gone, but because something else is being asked of us.

It takes intention to make space for them again... to step back into yourself without guilt... without apology... without the belief that caring for others requires disappearing completely.

What I see in her is the willingness to hold both…love for the life she has built… and the recognition that she is still fully present within it.

Not lost.

Not replaced.

Purely still here.

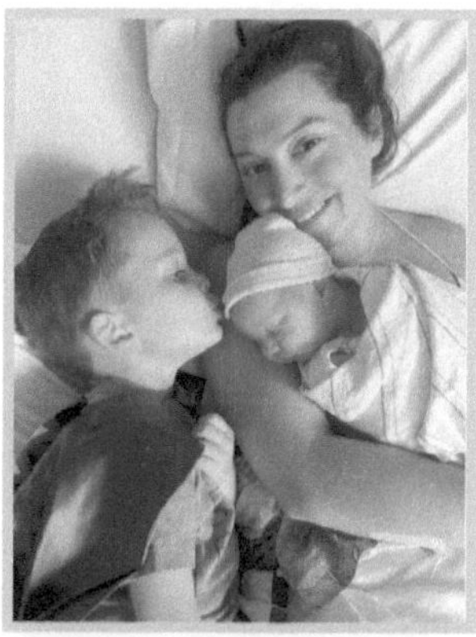

Da'Vontae Randolph
Player • Volunteer

2024

*"I had to stop playing as who I thought people would accept...
and start playing as myself."*

What does it cost a person to be fully seen... and what happens when they decide the cost of hiding is greater?

Da'Vontae does not talk about live reality games as if they are a hobby. He speaks about them as if they are a doorway... one that did not simply open, but altered him the moment he stepped through it. In 2020, masked and careful in the middle of a world that had slowed to uncertainty, he sat on a campus bench with people who were still strangers. The air carried distance. Every interaction felt measured. Nothing about that moment suggested transformation. It felt small. Contained. A quiet yes.

And still... it divided his life into before and after.

He did not arrive with a plan to be visible. He did not arrive seeking a platform or a voice. He arrived the way most people do—curious and cautious, hoping that what he stepped into would give more than it took. What he could not have known was that this doorway would widen him. It would ask more of him than strategy or endurance, and eventually, it would ask him to confront something far more difficult than losing.

It would ask him *to stop performing*.

Da'Vontae grew up navigating spaces where identity was never neutral. Poor. Black. In a small community, and later in larger ones where difference introduces itself before you have a chance to. In those spaces, awareness becomes instinct. You learn to monitor your tone. You learn to read reactions quickly. You learn that some mistakes are overlooked while others are remembered in ways that extend far beyond the moment itself.

So Da'Vontae learned to edit. Not out of preference. Out of necessity.

That instinct followed him into the LRG world. In many of the games he entered, he was often the only Black-presenting person in the cast or the crew. That reality is not symbolic. It is felt. It lives in the body. It sharpens attention. It adds weight to every interaction. There is a pause before speaking, a calculation before challenging something, an awareness that your presence may be read as representative even when you are simply being human.

What happened at his very first game is a thread that runs through the very essence of this book...

He showed up not as Da'Vontae, but as a version of himself he believed could win. A version shaped by experience. Designed for survival. Familiar... *but not entirely true.*

♦

The game ended. He drove back into Bloomington. Three days in the woods behind him. The city ahead. And somewhere on that road, something arrived that had nothing to do with placement.

"I wasn't sad that I lost," he told me. "I was sad that it wasn't me losing." His words live at center of everything.

Da'Vontae had gotten to the end of an experience that was supposed to reveal him, and he came out having revealed almost nothing real. The version that played that game was edited. Strategic. Preemptive. A performance that he understood from the inside even while others could not see it from the outside.

"I felt like I didn't really get to be a hundred percent myself," he said. "And all of it just flooded on me at once." What he felt sitting with that loss was not frustration about the game. It was grief for the self that had not shown up.

That grief would become the most important thing he carried out of the woods.

"The biggest lesson that I have taken from it," he said, "was just allowing myself to take my walls down." He paused thoughtfully, "Allowing myself to be me. And to be accepted and loved by these people regardless." Da'Vontae had spent years learning to protect himself by shrinking. That game finally showed him the cost of that protection.

◆

Another memory and pivotal moment for Da'Vontae was when a cast photo was released and he stood alone... the sole Black member. The absence did not strike him immediately. Not because it was right, but because it was familiar. This is the cast, he thought, the way someone does when they have learned not to expect more.

Some community members saw it differently. Messages came quickly. Calls followed. People he barely knew reached out with urgency, with concern, and some with frustration. Screens filled with notifications. Opinions arrived faster than clarity. Some asked questions. Some demanded answers. Many looked toward him for leadership.

Da'Vontae was still just someone who had applied to play a game... and at once, called to more. *Speak up about the cast and representation? Drop from the cast? Do nothing?*

That moment did not define him, but it revealed something to Da'Vontae. It showed him that this community could be more aware than the patterns it had inherited. That people were willing to sit inside discomfort rather than move around it. That something better was possible, even if it had not yet been built.

Later, when another cast was released without Black representation, he chose to speak. This time, he named the absence. He did not do it from a place of opposition. He did it from a place of care. He held the tension of loving something enough to challenge it, of believing in its potential while refusing to ignore its gaps. That is not criticism. That is ownership.

♦

Da'Vontae speaks about Diversity in a way many do not understand. He is keenly aware that inclusion does not happen on its own. It is not the natural result of good intentions. You cannot post an application and expect inclusion to find its way in. It requires effort. It requires intention followed by action. It requires going into spaces where people already exist and extending trust before expecting it in return.

Effort is the word he returns to because effort is what separates what we say from what we build.

He stepped into the creation of a new LRG alongside a team and served as the DEI coordinator and lead caster. He spent seven or eight months in that work, meeting twice a month, shaping the game from the ground up, and ensuring that the casting reflected the breadth and depth of the community.

"I was there to ensure that this game was going to be cast in a way that implemented DEI standards and represented everyone I could find," he said. "I just had such a wide range of people who were representing their cultures, their communities, and all of that."

He eventually stepped back from that project, but the seeds he planted lived on. The game found its host, Nicole Johnston, an Asian American woman and a fellow *Survival Challenge* alumna, someone who carries her own history of being seen and unseen in the same breath.

He is clear about what it means to build something rather than simply critique it. Da'Vontae has lived that process. He understands how quickly intention can stall without follow-through. He understands how fragile opportunity can be if no one is willing to hold it open long enough for someone else to walk through.

◆

Da'Vontae is not interested in recreating what already exists. He imagines games where everyone begins from the same place of unfamiliarity. Where no one enters with an advantage rooted in experience alone. Where discovery matters more than imitation. Where presence matters more than preparation.

He has ideas for original games, not *Survivor* remakes, but formats shaped by something different. Games rooted in fairness of origin, built from scratch, where the creator and the player are still figuring it out together. "I feel like there are enough *Survivor*-style games out there that they don't necessarily need Da'Vontae to host another one," he said with a quiet certainty. "I would love to host an original game."

He also carries a larger vision for LRG community. He imagines regional competitions, where games send their best players across state lines and fans show up carrying pride for their corner of the country. "A host in Maine gets their best ten players and a host in Pennsylvania gets their best ten players," he said, "and we do the first versus. Maine versus Pennsylvania. It's just the natural next step."

What isn't new is his dream to play *Survivor*. He has been offered other opportunities, other stages that could bring visibility in different ways. He has stepped back from them more than once, choosing to protect the dream that first mattered to him. It is not an easy choice. It requires patience. It requires belief. It requires the willingness to wait without losing direction.

He is not chasing attention. He is honoring something deeper. And the most important decision he has made has nothing to do with where he will play.

It is about *who* he will be when he does, because Da'Vontae has chosen to stop editing himself.

He has chosen to step out of the version of himself built for safety and into the version that feels true. That choice did not make the world easier. It did not remove complexity or erase the weight he carries in certain spaces.

It made him free. Freedom did not arrive through volume or visibility. It arrived through alignment. Through the decision to stand fully as himself, without filtering for comfort or expectation.

When that shift happened, everything else changed.

Not because the game changed... because he did.

My Lens Reframed

I am left reconsidering what it means to be present in a space... to be fully myself regardless of the cost. The quiet calculations... the awareness... the discipline it takes to not adjust, not shrink, not become more palatable in order to belong.

He does not move that way.

He stays rooted in who he is... not without awareness of the space around him, but without surrendering to it. And in doing so, he reveals something deeper about authenticity.

It is not automatic. It is a choice... made again and again... often in the moments where it would be easier to become less.

And that choice carries remarkable power and self-determination.

Presence alone does not change a space. What changes it is what someone chooses to carry into it... and what they refuse to leave behind. The decision to be fully yourself... not as an act of resistance alone... but as a commitment to something larger than the moment you are standing in.

There is a cost in that... in being the only... in holding your ground when it would be easier to adapt. But what I see in Da'Vontae is a refusal to let that cost define who he becomes.

Once he chose to stand fully in who he is... the space around him could not go unchanged.

To be fully present... is not only to exist within a space... It is to mold it.

To challenge what is missing... not by stepping away... but by building what should have been there in the first place.

WORDS OF WISDOM

"I learned that losing hurts less than hiding."

~ Da'Vontae Randolph

Part Four

Staying Is a Choice

After the rupture comes the decision. To leave. To harden. Or to stay. Staying is not passive. It is deliberate. It requires reflection, boundaries, and a deeper understanding of who you are when the noise fades. The individuals in this section did not ignore the cost of their experiences. They chose to return with greater clarity. Growth, in the end, is not about avoiding pain. It is about choosing to use it wisely.

"Be who you needed when you were younger."

~ Jaymes Lanoye

Amos Ray Smith

Player • Creator

2024

*"I didn't think my life was worth living... and now I can't
imagine it any other way."*

In a world filled with so many people who have an endless supply of
words, thoughts, and opinions, there are others who speak sparingly...
and still manage to draw people in. Amos belongs to the latter. The
remembered.

When we first spoke, I noticed it immediately. Amos did not rush to
fill space or perform insight for the sake of being heard. He spoke only
when something mattered, and when he did, it carried weight. It was
not volume that drew you in, but substance. As a storyteller, that kind
of presence is unmistakable, the kind that causes you to lean in without
even realizing you have done so.

Before we ever talked about games, I told Amos why he was here
and why his experience was vital to the essence of this book. During the
casting process for our LRG Documentary, Amos listened intently. I
remember watching him in the corner of my screen. Present. Observant.
Willing... but trusting and allowing his team to speak on behalf of

Surviving Reelfoot. I would later discover that he learned this over time —the well-earned lesson to lean on your circle of support.

I was immediately drawn to Amos by what he didn't say. A simple belief guides my listening: *true depth holds a sacred position*. That position is so pure, so whole—that it is willing to wait for those who seek it.

Amos listened, considered, and then nodded before sharing that he doesn't talk a lot, but that he is still open. "I'm a true extroverted introvert," he said, "so I don't speak a whole lot, but I'm still a very vulnerable person." The justaposition gave me a glimpse of the human, Amos. He is someone who is comfortable with people and energized by connection, yet deeply private about his inner world.

He grew up in a town so small it barely registers on a map, "a population of about 150 people... a whole eighth of a mile long. We don't even have a stop sign." This was a place where difference was noticed immediately and rarely welcomed.

Amos knew early on that he was different, though he did not yet have the language to name it. What he had instead was the feeling of standing just outside the circle. He remembered being "the kid that would sit on the swings and swing during recess and watch the other kids play games," never quite certain he belonged. That feeling followed him through playgrounds, classrooms, and conversations that never made room for him. Over time, he learned how to watch, how to read tone, posture, and silence, and how to sense whether a room was safe or not.

That quiet observation and emotional awareness would later become one of his greatest strengths.

Amos did not discover *Survivor* through television first. He found it through a video game, an interactive experience he stumbled across in 2004.

"I put it in my computer and I was hooked, absolutely hooked," he said. That doorway led him into online reality games, and those experiences led him to a realization that would quietly redirect his life. He began to wonder, "How cool would it be to do this in real life for a weekend?"

The idea stayed with him and took root over time. It began as a simple one-day experiment with friends, using folding tables, handwritten votes, and borrowed space. Then it expanded into an overnight game with higher stakes and deeper connections. Eventually, it became something larger, something structured, intentional, and demanding.

By 2014, *Surviving Reelfoot* existed.

◆

At that time, Amos was at one of the lowest points in his life. He was struggling financially, emotionally depleted, and questioning whether his life held any lasting value.

He told me plainly that he did not know if he wanted to keep going. "This isn't the life I want to live," he remembered thinking. "If I have to live another 60, 70 years like this, I don't want to do it."

Then people showed up.

They came to play, but they also came to be seen. They told Amos that the game mattered, and that *he mattered*. They told him that what he had built gave them something they did not realize they were missing until they experienced it. They found laughter around campfires, arguments that eventually led to understanding, and strangers who left feeling like something closer to family.

People began telling him, "You did something great," and later, and even more powerful, "You changed my life."

In the midst of that, something in Amos began to flow in a new direction.

◆

Surviving Reelfoot did not grow by accident. Amos built it deliberately, season by season, rule by rule, and boundary by boundary. Early mistakes taught him difficult lessons. He micromanaged at times. He tried to control outcomes. He carried stress in ways he didn't know how to release.

Looking back, he was honest about it: "The first few seasons, it's not something I'm proud of."

Over time, his leadership evolved.

Structure became a form of care. "I don't do well with chaos," he said. "I have to be very structured with stuff." Clear expectations, firm boundaries, consistency, and trust in his team began to shape the experience. He also learned to trust the process and to understand that mistakes were not failures, but opportunities for growth. Where he once felt everything "has to be this way," he learned instead, "Okay, we will work around this and let it go."

Surviving Reelfoot expanded from a small experiment into a multi-day experience set across hundreds of acres. The land itself became part of the story, open stretches, dense woods that swallowed sound, and paths shaped by seasons of players carrying hope and hunger into the environment. People began traveling not only from across the country, but from around the world to participate.

They did not come for prize money or for fame. They came for belonging. They came to be challenged. They came to test themselves. They came to grow.

Amos did not only build games. He stepped into them as a player. When he speaks about gameplay, he recalls details with remarkable clarity, the votes, the conversations, and the subtle shifts in loyalty. He understands strategy instinctively, yet he is honest about his own challenges.

"I'm not a very good public speaker," he admitted, and he knows that playing well does not guarantee a win.

His experiences as a player changed how he hosted. It gave him a deeper sense of empathy and perspective. He became more patient with mistakes, more intentional about fairness, and more protective of the emotional experience of the players. He understood the stakes not as theory, but as something lived, the tension of waiting to hear your name, the relief when it is not called, and the quiet that follows elimination when adrenaline fades and reality settles in.

He told me he became, "one of the easiest people to host because I know what it's like," and that understanding shaped the way he now cares for others in his game.

When Amos told me that creating *Surviving Reelfoot* saved his life, the look in his eyes spoke volumes. I could almost journey back with him to the time and place where he thought endings his life was an option. He spoke about growing up gay in a place that had no language to support his identity. He spoke about internalized prejudice, about loneliness, and about the slow erosion of self-worth that happens when a person never feels chosen.

"I didn't feel wanted," he said simply. Over time, difference begins to feel like defect.

Surviving Reelfoot gave him something to build toward, and in building it, he rebuilt himself.

"I went from, *this isn't worth it* and *how am I going to end this...* to *now I'm married and I have a beautiful family and I have kids.*" Then he said the words that still linger with me: "*Survivor* in general... it changed my life, but *Surviving Reelfoot*, it saved my life."

As his world expanded, so did his understanding. Meeting people from different cultures, identities, and experiences reshaped the way he saw others and himself.

He unlearned beliefs he had once accepted and grew into advocacy, not because it was popular, but because it was necessary. "I had to unlearn a lot of bad things in my life," he shared, and that unlearning became part of his becoming.

When I asked Amos why LRGs affect people so deeply, his answer was simple and grounded in experience.

There is no escape. There are no phones, no distractions, and no buffers. People suffer together, celebrate together, and fail together.

"You're hungry together, you're competing together, you're strategizing together," he said. Vulnerability becomes unavoidable. The weather is real. The hunger is real. The disappointment is real. And so is the laughter that breaks through it.

In that environment, Amos explained, people begin to see themselves more clearly. They begin to understand who they are and who they have the potential to become.

As Amos put it perfectly, some people come out there and realize amazing things about themselves, "I didn't even know I could do this."

For Amos, the healing is found in reflection. It lives in the quiet hours after the camp settles, in the moments when a person realizes they are stronger than they believed, and in the understanding that community can form where none existed before.

He described it as "a lot of self-reflection," the kind that strips life down until a person can finally feel and know "what's important."

It is in those moments that a person begins to see that they are not alone.

My Lens Reframed

Amos' story is not simply about a game created in the woods. It is about what happens when creation becomes a lifeline... when building something for others gives someone a reason to stay.

- did not come from abundance. It came from need... from loneliness... from a life searching for something that could hold. That origin matters. It changes how I understand what was built... not as something optional, but as something necessary.

Creation, in this context, is not driven by inspiration alone. It is driven by survival. By the decision to build something meaningful in the absence of it... and to continue building even when the outcome is uncertain... even when there is no guarantee that it will reach beyond the person creating it.

And what begins there does not stay contained.

Some things are built so people can keep going. What begins in need can become something that holds others... something that extends beyond the person who first imagined it.

Through Amos, I came to understand that creation can be a lifeline... not only for the one who builds it, but for the people who find themselves inside what has been made. What began in loneliness becomes something shared. What began as need becomes structure... and that structure, in turn, becomes care.

Lives are steadied here.

Reshaped, not by accident, but by intention... by the decision to create a space where people can arrive as they are and find something that holds.

And there is something deeper moving underneath it all...

People are not fixed. What we have been taught can be unlearned.Pain does not have the final word.

Sometimes, the bravest thing a person can do is press on... uncertain... but willing to see what lies ahead.

Some games are played to win.

Others are created so that people can continue living.

Keenan Lucas
Player • Host

2026

*"These games don't just connect players... they build bridges
between lives that would never have crossed."*

Keenan speaks the way some people breathe after running... with quick
turns, half laughter, and thoughts arriving just ahead of punctuation.
There is an energy in him that does not settle easily, a forward motion
that feels constant. When we first began talking, he did not start with
the game. He started with time.

He described 2020 as a beginning. A new year, a new decade, and a
version of himself that was ready to step forward. None of us knew
what that year would bring, but he knew that if he was going to move
into whatever came next, he wanted to do it fully.

◆

Survivor existed in fragments inside him long before he stepped into
the woods. He remembered jungle shots, water challenges, contestants
submerged beneath wooden grates and holding their breath in ways that
felt almost impossible. As a child, swimming was not easy for him.

Submersion was not something that felt calm or cinematic. It was overwhelming, loud, and disorienting.

Watching people remain composed underwater did not feel like entertainment. It felt like confrontation.

Keenan found himself asking how they were able to do it, and instead of turning away, he leaned closer. Fear did not push him back. It drew him in.

By 2020, *Survivor* had become a kind of compass. He saw *Survivor BC* appear in his feed and initially assumed it must be scripted. It felt too raw, too earnest, too unpolished to be real. Still, curiosity stayed with him. He watched one episode, then another, and before long he was fully immersed.

Then he applied.

When the host sent a message asking if he was still interested, the dates had been shifted by the pandemic. The final day of his seventy five day fitness challenge was July 14th. The game began July 16th.

"Truth be told," Keenan said, "if that season overlapped the fitness challenge I was doing, I would've said no."

He paused after saying it, the way people pause when they recognize how much depends on timing they did not control. In the actual game of *Survivor*, luck is real. In Live Reality Games, it is just as real. His luck held. He said yes. And two days after completing the most physically demanding commitment he had ever made to himself, he stepped into his first live game.

Keenan is clear about how he enters these experiences. "Every game I've played, I have the goal to win," he said. "I don't have a desire to do anything lower."

That is not arrogance. It is intention. He does not enter anything halfway.

In his first game, that intensity was visible immediately. He made bold reads, formed quick alliances, and took calculated risks. Then came the challenge. A live-streamed reward competition. Whoever could create the longest chain from whatever was on their body would win.

"I would do whatever it takes to win this game, even strip," he said. "So, there was my stripping. I stripped for the tribe." Keenan removed every item of clothing. On a live stream. With a full cast watching.

He was not ashamed of his body. He had spent seventy five days earning it back. He was also playing a metaphor in real time, showing the tribe what he would sacrifice, hoping it would register when the game reached its final calculations. It was youth meeting adrenaline, a moment where inhibition gave way to instinct.

He placed sixth. He learned quickly. What he carried out of that experience was not pride. It was awareness.

◆

The woods amplify everything. Excitement becomes louder. Paranoia sharpens. Ego and doubt both rise to the surface. For Keenan, something else emerged as well.

He began to see how his neurodivergence shaped the way he experienced social dynamics. In early games, he would feel as though he was part of conversations that he was actually orbiting. He interpreted trust generously and assumed alignment where there was still uncertainty.

The realization that you were not fully included does not arrive dramatically. It shows up in subtle ways, in pauses, in tone, in the shift of energy when you enter a space.

That experience stayed with him. It was not exactly rejection. It was the recognition of having misread a moment.

He began to notice how intensely he processed social interactions, how conversations replayed in his mind, how tone and expression carried weight beyond the moment itself. At first, this felt like an obstacle.

Over time, it became something else.

It became a tool.

He developed discernment. Not simply whether to trust, *but who* to trust. Not whether to be open, *but when*. He stopped leading with immediate vulnerability and began to lead with observation.

"I'm finding out who the right people to tell are," he said. "I don't just go swinging out of the bat with it. I give a good time to discuss it."

The biggest lesson of his first season came through in a sentence so simple it almost sounds obvious. But most of us spend years learning it.

"Just be the person you are," he said. "Be your wholehearted self, the genuine person you are, and the right people will enter your life. The people that are meant to stick with you will stick."

He said it with the steadiness of someone who has tested it under real pressure and found it to be true.

◆

As Keenan moved between games in Canada and the United States, across different formats and communities, he began to see the ecosystem more clearly.

He brought his father into a Blood vs. Water season, sharing not only the experience but the strategy, watching someone with almost no *Survivor* knowledge navigate a world built entirely on the language of the game. He crossed borders that did not always cooperate with his plans. He experienced what happens when the game expands beyond placement and into connection.

At some point, the goal shifted. It did not move away from winning, but it expanded beyond it.

When I asked him why people do this at all, why they pay to suffer, why they travel across the country to sleep in the woods and compete, his answer came fast.

"Passion," he said. "Absolute passion. Living the dream of their favorite show. It's the closest most are going to get."

And then he said something that I have returned to more than once since our conversation.

"The power of live reality games," Keenan said, "really comes from exhilarating that passion and allowing it to become an infinite bridge between communities for life. It does exactly what real *Survivor* does, brings people from different parts of the country, the continent, hell, the world—and it builds a permanent bridge between societies."

He eventually stepped into hosting in support friends who worked to create *Surviving Canada*. This charity-based game supporting the *Mission Youth Center*, was a worthy Keenan didn't hesitate to come alongside.

Standing at the edge of the field, watching players navigate the structure he helped build, gave him a different perspective. He was able to see the entire system. Not just his role within it.

◆

I asked him directly whether the two things could exist in the same space. Playing hard. Playing to win. And still leaving with something real.

"It sure as bloody hell could coexist," he said, without a pause.

He framed it like a boxing match. When you step into the ring, both people know they will be hit. The agreement is mutual. What breaks trust is pretending the match is something it is not.

The people who struggle with that coexistence, he said, are often those who cannot separate the feeling of being outmaneuvered from the act of being betrayed. That is a harder thing to navigate. He does not judge it. He has felt it. But he does not let it close him off.

"No matter how well you place," he said, "no matter how far you go, the blunders you make along the way, the good things you do along the way—you will meet a lot of good people and it becomes the bonding experience of a lifetime. You're meeting people just as crazy and passionate as yourself."

At twenty nine, approaching thirty, Keenan carries a steadier rhythm. The space between his thoughts has widened. The hunger is still there, but it is no longer frantic. It is directed.

He understands that most players will never appear on *CBS Survivor*, and that realization does not diminish these games. It deepens their meaning. Live Reality Games are not secondary experiences. They are spaces where growth is tested, where identity is shaped, and where people are given the opportunity to engage fully with themselves and with others.

You can want to win. You can compete with intensity. And you can still build something that lasts beyond you.

When I think of Keenan now, I do not think about a single moment or a placement. I think about someone standing at the edge of something he helped build, watching others step into it with the same intensity he once carried, and recognizing that the structure is strong enough to hold them.

My Lens Reframed

Keenan reminded me that intensity is not a problem... only intensity left unexamined.

When hunger is paired with reflection, it becomes something else entirely. It turns into fuel... something directed... something intentional... rather than something that consumes.

It changed how I think about competition.

It is not about domination. It is about commitment... about being willing to engage fully... to bring everything you have into the moment without losing connection to yourself in the process.

That kind of engagement requires awareness. It asks you to understand what is driving you... to recognize when intensity is sharpening you... and when it is pulling you away from who you are.

And what I see in him is a kind of discernment that is not immediate... but learned. Built through experience... through moments where something had to be faced, understood, and carried differently the next time.

I am left with the image of someone who once feared submersion... now standing steady within it. Not only able to remain... but able to guide others across.

Keenan plays to win.

But what he is building is something stronger.

He is building something that holds... a path that others can step onto... and trust that it will carry them forward.

FRANCES DIEDERICH
PLAYER • CREATOR

2024

"I do not make my decisions with my emotions... I make them with my brain while crying about it."

What happens when someone who learned to survive by adapting decides to trust herself enough to lead?

That question stayed with me as I listened to Frances speak... as I watched them move through the game... as I traced the shape of her story both backward and forward. Her answer did not arrive all at once. It revealed itself slowly—season by season, online, then in person, then somewhere deeper than the game itself. First in small shifts. Then in choices that felt almost invisible at the time. And eventually, in a presence that no longer asked permission to exist.

Frances' story does not begin in the woods.

It begins in the glow of a screen—late at night—inside the fierce, loyal world of online reality games, where you learn the game in public and learn yourself in private.

"I started with ORGs when I was about nineteen or twenty," they told me. "I fell completely in love with it."

Her first love was a *Survivor*-format series called *Can You Survive?* It didn't just entertain her—it claimed her. She played three times. Helped host multiple seasons. Stayed up long after she should have, thinking through decisions that would not land until hours later. And at some point, the line between playing and becoming blurred.

There is a moment she carries permanently—one that tells you everything about who she is. Faced with a choice between safety and sacrifice during an *All Stars* challenge, she chose pain over panic. She marked that decision not as decoration, but as evidence.

Frances does not approach intensity lightly. They trust it. They will take the harder road if it keeps them in the fight.

♦

Eventually, the online world reached forward and grabbed the real one. The host of *Can You Survive?* wanted to bring his ORG into physical space. Frances was supposed to play the first season. Health issues intervened. She applied for season two—and was denied.

"I was really mad about it," they said. But she listened. The host told her plainly that there were dynamics in that cast she wouldn't want to step into. When she later saw the lineup, she understood. She respected the players—but trusted the warning.

Sometimes rejection isn't failure. It's protection. The door didn't end the story.

It rerouted it.

♦

Later came a season that would turn her LRG life into something she would carry permanently.

Blood vs. Water.

Frances' mom is a longtime *Survivor* fan—social, charming, competitive, the kind of woman who could win an endurance challenge and then convince you to hand over your jacket afterward. Frances didn't gently introduce her to live reality games.

"We're applying right now," she remembered saying—immediate, certain, already in motion.

The timing felt almost scripted—July 2023, three days after Frances' birthday. The game met them fully. Heat that lingered. Rain on the second day that did not let up. Clothes that never quite dried.

"I don't think I've ever cried that much in a four-day period," they said, almost surprised by their own honesty.

Somewhere in the middle of that experience, she thought: *Why would I ever do this again?*

Two days after that game ended, the craving arrived and Frances wanted to know when the next game would be!

◆

Blood vs. Water gave her one of the most unforgettable moments in her LRG story. Frances—fully undone—held up a vote. For her own mother.

There is a photograph of it. Hazy. Raw. Unmistakable. It captures the strange sacred tension of these games: the moment when strategy collides with love... and the game does not flinch.

"I was sobbing... but I still did it," they said. They made the choice. And then they lived inside it.

That is where something shifted. "I marched up that hill," they told me, "and I turned my game on."

◆

Online-Frances moves with confidence. She understands structure. She can navigate alliances. She can think multiple steps ahead.

"I could run a tribe," they said simply. But live play asked something different of her. It asked her to stand inside herself—without distance.

Frances lives with social anxiety. In large groups, her body responds before her thoughts can catch up. In that first live game, her mother became her bridge—not symbolically, but practically. Building connections. Creating space. Helping her move through an unfamiliar environment.

"She made my alliances for me," Frances said, still half-laughing at how true it was. But the game does what it always does... it removes safety.

When Frances found herself outside of a vote—not eliminated, but not included—she faced a choice that would define her. Not in theory. In action. Shrink or sharpen?

She chose to sharpen.

That choice did not come from nowhere. Frances is a lesbian who spent thirteen years in Christian school. She says it plainly: *you learn survival skills in places that don't always know what to do with you.* You learn to read rooms. You learn timing. You learn how to protect softness without surrendering strength.

Those skills did not disappear in the mud and rain of live play. They transformed. What began as survival became strategy. What was once protection became awareness. *What was once adaptation became leadership.*

When the vote finally came that forced her to write her mother's name down, Frances entered the merge as one of only two players without a loved one. The other became her anchor. She adapted fast. Bonded deeply. Refused to collapse.

She didn't win *Blood vs. Water*. She came close—final juror, only one vote cast against her the entire game. The person who finally clocked her threat level was the person she trusted most. Her ally won final immunity, voted her out, and saw her clearly.

Frances doesn't resent that moment. She respects it.

By the time Frances arrived to play again, something inside her had settled. Not the absence of fear—but a different relationship with it. She no longer allowed it to decide how she would show up.

What's striking is that most people would never know. They read as present, engaged, bright—confident. Delightful, even. That is not because fear is gone. It is because she has learned how to move with it.

Frances uses she and they pronouns, and she moves through the game with intention. She understands what people expect to see and how quickly those expectations become assumptions. In earlier games, she leaned into femininity—pink hair, curated softness—because she understood how assumptions work. If someone wanted to underestimate her, she was willing to let them.

And then beat them with it.

"If they think I'm an emotional crybaby girl... that's fine," they said. "I make my decisions with my brain... while crying about it."

There is quiet power in that. Emotion is not the opposite of strategy. It is part of it. She can feel deeply and still think clearly. She can cry and still calculate. She can hold tenderness and precision at the same time.

That is not contradiction. That is capacity.

◆

One of her most meaningful experiences came from a game designed with intention—one that split tribes by identity: he, she, they, gays.

What could have become spectacle became something rare instead: *space.*

Her "they" tribe was filled with other players who used they/them pronouns. No translation required. No preface necessary. They dominated—five "theys" reached the Final Eight. The final three were all thems.

"It was so cool," she said simply.

It removed the need to explain. To monitor. To compress. It allowed her to exist fully, without adjustment. And when a host sets the table with that kind of care, the game becomes a place where people don't just survive—*they breathe.*

◆

Now Frances is building worlds of her own... *The Frances Franchise.*

Her first hosted LRG is a one-day indoor game in Columbus, adapted from a format she once ran online. After playing a one-day mini game, she fell in love with the vibe—quick, chaotic, joyful. Players going hard but still laughing.

She didn't open casting publicly. "I just invited people," she said—choosing care over scale. She filled fourteen spots and closed the moment she hit her number. She didn't want to reject anyone.

That choice makes a statement. She is competitive—but careful with people.

And then the full-circle moment arrived quietly: her mom will play again. This time, in Frances' game.

The daughter who once sobbed while voting out her mother is now building a world her mother will step into.

You can't manufacture that arc. You earn it by saying yes—again and again.

♦

Before we ended our conversation, Frances handed me something unexpected.

I told them about a dream I've carried—an LRG designed for women who feel overlooked, quietly convinced that life has already passed them by. I admitted I'd hesitated.

Frances didn't flinch.

They told me what three days in an LRG did for their mother. How it grew her confidence. How it followed her home. How it changed the shape of her life.

They said—gently, clearly—that they didn't think their mom would have called a divorce lawyer if she hadn't played that first game.

Because the game didn't give her mom a title.

It gave her space, a voice, and permission...

If you've ever wondered why this community matters—that's why.

MY LENS REFRAMED

Frances widened how I understand adaptation.

What begins as survival does not have to remain there. When it is nurtured... when it is trusted... it becomes something more.

It becomes strategy.
It becomes awareness.
It becomes leadership rooted in care.

Something learned in necessity can evolve. Instinct becomes awareness... and awareness, when trusted, becomes something you can use with intention... not only to move through a system, but to shape it.

That kind of trust does not arrive all at once.

It builds... in moments where you allow yourself to feel fully... even when your hands are shaking... where you let emotion move through you without letting it stop you. Not as a contradiction to strength... but as part of it. As information... as signal... as something to be understood rather than pushed aside.

What once looked like hesitation becomes action. What once felt uncertain becomes something you can stand inside of.

Frances carries something rare.

The ability to feel deeply... and still move forward.

And when the next moment arrives... they do not wait for permission.

They step into it... fully... and they go.

Jacob Burklow-Rogers

Player • Volunteer

2024

"I'm half game-bot."

What happens when someone stops studying the game from a distance... and steps inside it, willing to let it change how they see everything... including themselves?

Jacob does not simply watch *Survivor*. He lives inside it. Not in the way people sometimes assume, where knowledge is measured by statistics or trivia, but in a way that moves beneath the surface. When he talks about the game, he is not recounting events. He is unraveling them. He slows moments down. He rewinds decisions. He looks at a vote and asks what was felt before it was written. He studies not just the move, but the motive... not just the outcome, but the pressure that shaped it.

That kind of attention is a true devotion to understanding.

♦

Survivor was never separate from his life. It existed in the background first, something woven into the rhythm of his home. The television on. His family watching. Voices rising and falling with the energy of the game. At first, it was something he caught in fragments. A challenge here. A moment of tension there. Then slowly, it became something more complete.

"It became family night where we'd watch *Survivor* together," Jacob smiled. "I was already a nature boy, a survival boy—somebody who wanted to go out into the woods and camp and build a fort. It just worked perfectly."

One of his earliest memories is not just of a season, but of a moment that expanded what the game could be. An unexpected proposal during a live reunion... *Rob and Amber*. Emotion layered over competition. The realization that what was unfolding was not contained to a single episode or a single outcome added depth to Jacob's love for the experience. The game was a story that continued long after the votes were read.

Rupert also became a figure who felt both larger than life, and yet strangely familiar. A presence rooted in the outdoors, in survival, in something physical and grounded. "Rupert was so good at fishing and he was so good at the survival stuff and the challenges," Jacob recalled, "that he brought in a seven-year-old kid and gave me someone to relate to and root for."

For a young boy who loved the woods, who built and climbed and explored, Rupert was not just someone to watch. He was someone to recognize.

Years later, that recognition became real. A meeting at a local festival. The smell of food in the air. Booths lining the path. A moment where someone who had once lived only on a screen became tangible.

"I ended up meeting him just a few years later at the Earth Day Festival," Jacob said, with the quiet pleasure of someone still surprised by the memory. "He signed my Earth Day book."

◆

When Jacob calls himself a super-fan, there is no hesitation. The word fits, but he defines it carefully.

"A super fan is somebody who deep dives into something—who wants to learn every nook and cranny of the situation," he said. "The strategy behind it, the numbers behind it, why a person had that motivation to make that move. A casual viewer turns it on Wednesday night and doesn't think about it too much the rest of the week. A super fan is living in it all week."

Jacob did not study the game for trivia... he studied it for humanity.

That study expanded through conversation and community. Online spaces filled with people who spoke the same language. Podcasts that extended the life of each episode. Hours spent listening, not for answers, but for perspective. For the why beneath the what.

And slowly... that perspective began to shape how he saw the world beyond the game.

Jacob is a learner at his core. A former teacher. A person who finds energy in understanding something deeply enough to share it with others. His life reflects that curiosity. Time spent outdoors. An appreciation for the small and intricate details of the natural world. A love for rocks that becomes something far more than a hobby. He carries that same curiosity into people.

Family is central. The ritual of watching together, even as life shifts and schedules change. A shared language that continues to evolve. It is not just about the show. It is about connection.

◆

For a long time, Jacob stood just outside the edge of participation. Close enough to understand. Close enough to imagine what it would feel like. Not yet willing to step fully into it. There is a particular kind of fear that comes with turning something you love into something you might fail at. Watching is safe. Analyzing is safe. Playing asks something different.

It asks you to risk being seen.

It took time before he said yes. Even then, it was not a bold, decisive moment. It was something quieter—an alternate slot, a last-minute need, a door that opened just wide enough. "The only way I was going to say yes was because, oh, someone else needs me," he said. "I'm not doing it for myself. They need a spot filled. Alright, great."

The experience was immediate and overwhelming. Conversations moving quickly. Decisions stacking on top of each other. Strategy unfolding in real time. It was everything he had studied... and completely different when lived.

He was blindsided.

"It's a badge of honor to get idoled out," he said afterward, "but it made my experience a lot more difficult to want to jump into again. Because I'm like—*these are my dreams.* And if I'm just going to fail at my dreams... I might just want to have the hope forever that I could do it."

There is a kind of clarity that comes from that moment. A sharp awareness that understanding something intellectually is not the same as experiencing it emotionally. The lesson does not arrive gently. It lands. For a time, it made Jacob question whether he wanted to return.

And then... *he did.*

The drive to Massachusetts was fourteen and a half hours. That number is not incidental. It is the measure of commitment—hours on the road, space to think, the slow recognition that he was stepping into something that would ask more of him than before. He did not go only to compete... he went to understand.

Live Reality Games offer something that cannot be replicated elsewhere. They compress time. They accelerate connection. They create environments where people reveal themselves quickly—not because they intend to, but because the conditions make it unavoidable. Jacob is fascinated by that.

"The competitions, the challenges were so cool," he said. "I used to be an athlete. I don't get to be an athlete anymore, so I get to be competitive again. I get to try to win, I get to try to make myself proud in that way." He paused. "But this is also a people game. It's a social experiment. And so I'm fascinated by the way people work together— the way people rub in the right ways and rub in the wrong ways."

He understands that strategy is never purely logical. Emotion enters. Relationships complicate decisions. What should happen and what does happen rarely align perfectly. That tension is where meaning lives.

◆

LRGs have changed Jacob.

"I think they have made me into a better human," Jacob said. "More empathetic. It allows you to think about other people's perspectives from their shoes—and you have to really try to get to know them as you play to understand that." He does not separate the game from the person. He sees both.

These experiences have shifted how he sees people. They have made him more hopeful, not less. They have shown him that when individuals are placed in an environment that requires presence, something real emerges. Not always clean. Not always easy. But real.

"You take a pool of strangers and they're actually a lot nicer than you might think," he said. "This kind of game makes you break down those walls and makes you be vulnerable. You truly learn who you are because you're being vulnerable. And you truly learn who they are because they're being vulnerable."

◆

Jacob does not know exactly what comes next, but he does know this: *he will not remain the same.*

He is not interested in repeating himself. He is interested in expanding—trying something different, playing in ways that challenge his instincts rather than reinforce them.

"If I played the hero the first time, why not try to be the villain?" he said, with a half-smile in his voice. "Make it entertaining. Because at the end of the day you'll look back on it for a long time, and you want to enjoy it."

He has already set his sights beyond LRGs. "These kinds of games show you what you're made of," Jacob said. "They show you what kinds of emotions you'll go through. I feel way more prepared because of LRGs." That is not a small thing. That is the whole point.

◆

When I asked what he most wants readers to take from his story, the answer was immediate.

"The world is diverse and we need everyone from every walk of life who is capable of playing these games," he said. "And even if you don't think you're capable, you probably are. Where there's a will, there's a way. What you put in is what you get out. If you put in your heart, if you put in that love for the game, that's going to be given back to you twice fold—if not ten times."

Jacob paused, but I could see he was still thinking. Then he continued, "You're either building walls or breaking them. You can become more closed-minded as life goes on, or you can become more open-minded—but it's in the work that you do... and what you decide to do with it."

That is growth. That is commitment. That is Jacob.

My Lens Reframed

Jacob reminded me that understanding is not a destination. It is a practice. It requires curiosity, patience, and a willingness to sit with complexity rather than reduce it too quickly.

He does not approach the game to prove something. He approaches it to learn... and in doing so, he expands what the game can teach. And it reframes how I think about understanding itself.

It is not something we arrive at once and keep. It is something we return to... again and again... choosing to stay with what is not immediately clear... allowing meaning to deepen instead of rushing toward conclusion.

What I see in Jacob is an attentiveness to what lives beneath the surface... an awareness that every decision carries intention, even when that intention is not immediately visible. And it invites something different.

Not only to observe more carefully... but to engage more fully. To step beyond watching and into participation... even when the outcome is uncertain... even when answers are not guaranteed.

Because what changes is not only how we move through the experience...

It is how we see. And once that shifts... everything we encounter begins to open in a different way.

ERIC ELDREDGE

PLAYER • VIDEOGRAPHER

2024

"I learned more from how people reacted to me... than anything I thought I knew about myself."

Some people enter this world through the game. They arrive with strategy, with hunger, with a need to test themselves against others. Eric entered differently. He entered through the lens. Before he was known as a player or a personality, he was already watching... already paying attention to the things many people miss. A camera in his hand, a quiet posture, an awareness that did not need to announce itself in order to be felt.

I met him not as someone trying to be seen, but as someone already seeing. Even in conversation, that presence carries. He did not rush, did not overfill space. When he speaks, it is measured, often reflective.

"I had some preconceived notions... I thought these were kind of lame," he admitted when talking about LRGs—a quiet honesty that reveals how carefully he considers his own experience before offering it outward.

There is a patience to the way Eric moves through a space. He does not rush. He does not position himself as essential. He allows the moment to unfold before deciding where he belongs within it. That kind of restraint is easy to overlook. It reads as quiet. It reads as background.

It is neither. It is intention.

In a world where many people arrive with visible needs—hunger for connection, for recognition, for validation—Eric's posture stands apart. He is not searching for the moment that will elevate him. He is watching for the moment that reveals something true. The most important parts of the story rarely arrive fully formed. They flicker into existence. They live in the margins—in the pause after a handshake, in the hesitation before a vote, in the silence that lingers just long enough to say what someone is trying not to.

There is a discipline required to witness something honestly. It is not passive. It is the decision to be present without immediately shaping what unfolds. Eric holds that line with care.

As a videographer, he occupies a space that is both inside and outside the experience. Close enough to hear what is not being said out loud. Close enough to notice when something shifts before anyone acknowledges it. And yet he does not interrupt a fragile exchange to capture a better angle. He does not prompt emotion to make it more visible. He does not push a moment beyond what it naturally offers.

He understands that once you begin to shape the moment for the sake of the story, you risk losing the truth of it entirely.

He notices who stands just outside the center of the frame. He allows reactions to land before moving on. If something is awkward, he lets it be awkward. If something is tender, he gives it space. He understands that transformation is uneven. It is quiet. It is often difficult to watch.

That steadiness creates something rare. People relax around him. Vulnerability does not feel extracted or exposed. It feels witnessed. There is a difference between being observed and being seen. Eric understands that difference, and he honors it.

In spaces that reward amplification—where bigger often feels better, where the temptation to heighten what is already intense can be difficult to resist—Eric resists it. Not out of hesitation, but out of conviction. The story does not need to be made larger. It needs to be held carefully enough that it can remain intact.

He moves between roles with a fluidity that few people achieve. He understands what it means to be a player... the vulnerability of being read incorrectly, the sting of being voted out, the fragile hope that lives inside every decision. He understands production... the weight of long days, the unpredictability of the environment, the pressure to capture something meaningful without losing control of the process.

And yet, there is another layer to Eric that reveals itself when he steps into the game rather than observing it. He is not immune to discovery. In fact, he is shaped by it.

"I really thought of myself as a pretty unassuming guy," he said, reflecting on his early games, "but I found I was targeted very quickly... people perceive me as a huge threat. I found I was a lot louder and more extroverted than I thought I was being." He paused. "I've had a couple guys come up to me after a game and say: I wanted nothing to do with you the second I saw you. But then we got to talking, and you weren't that bad. That took me by surprise."

The gap between the person we believe we are presenting and the person others are receiving is one of the sharpest lessons these games offer. Eric filed it away not with defensiveness, but with curiosity.

"It's so hard to explain this hobby to people," he said, almost laughing at the absurdity of it. "I'm going to go willingly sleep on the ground in the woods and eat nothing and play a manipulative backstabbing game with friends and future enemies—and oh by the way, I'm also going to pay money to do that." He smiled. "But it's surprising how many people try this on a whim and they love the LRG experience. There's a common theme about learning about yourself.

I've learned a ton about myself—how I'm perceived and how I come off."

That level self-knowledge is vital to personal growth and building community. "A huge draw for LRGs is the sense of community," he explained. "A lot of us are big fans of these shows and there aren't that many of us out there in the real world. A lot of people have said: I've loved this show for years, maybe I watched it with my family, and I don't have anyone to talk about it with. And then this community is like, oh my god, this exists. You've got watch parties. It feels like watching the NBA Finals. That's a huge realization for some people—oh, there's a lot of other nerds out there I can talk about these games with."

That is not a small thing to give someone. The realization that the thing you love—the thing you may have watched alone for years without anyone to share it with—has an entire nation waiting for you inside it. Eric understands the power of that. He has lived it. And it shapes the care he brings to every frame he captures.

◆

Eric is pursuing something larger now. A master's degree in game design. The production side of reality television. A specific and studied understanding of how games work, why they work, and what they cost the people inside them.

"Interviewing people is my favorite part by far," he said. "I love talking to people and thinking about the big storylines and making people shine. That's where I would love to get involved."

He is not describing a career path. He is describing a calling.

The things Eric loves most—the craft of the interview, the architecture of a story, the moment a person relaxes enough to say what they actually mean—are the same things that make him exceptional in every role he steps into. As a videographer. As a player. As a presence inside a community that is still learning what it can become.

And that kind of presence changes more than a single moment... it shapes how a community remembers itself.

MY LENS REFRAMED

Eric reshaped how I understand visibility. Influence does not always belong to the loudest voice or the most central figure. Sometimes it belongs to the person who chooses to observe with care... who allows the story to remain whole rather than reshaping it to fit expectation.

That kind of observation is not passive.

It is a choice... one that preserves what is real rather than reducing it into something easier to hold. There is responsibility in that kind of presence... in deciding how closely you are willing to pay attention... and what you are willing to leave untouched.

Because the way something is witnessed becomes the way it is remembered.

And that space... between what happens and how it is carried forward... matters more than we often realize. It is where meaning settles. Where truth is either held or altered.

Integrity lives there.

Not always visible... but unmistakable in how something feels when it is told honestly... without distortion... without omission.

And what stays with me is this...

What lives on, long after the noise fades, is not only the event... but the story that was kept intact.

Long after the game ends... after the torches are gone... after everything quiets... what remains... is the story.

Melanie Bartlett
Player • LRG Casting
Page Creator • Volunteer

2024

What happens when a story ends before it ever really begins... and what drives someone to stay, build, and embrace?

I kept returning to that question. Not the dramatic exits or the players who leave with momentum behind them. Not the ones whose stories are framed, edited, and remembered. I was thinking about the quieter endings... the ones that happen before trust has time to form, before alliances take shape, before the game has a chance to see who someone really is.

Melanie's story answered that question, though not in the way I expected. It unfolded slowly, through what she chose to do after a game had already decided she was done.

Her first live reality game was a one-day game, *Survivor Philly,* Season One. She was voted out at her very first tribal council. There were no alliances to hold onto, no strategic conversations to replay, no sense of having fully entered the experience before it ended. The game moved on without her almost as quickly as it had begun.

Melanie chose to stay for the entire day anyway. She watched. She listened. She sat beside people who were still playing and those who had already been voted out. She showed up to the after-game gatherings, the pizza runs, the conversations in parking lots where the real stories begin to stretch and settle. She placed herself inside the space even after the game had removed her from it.

What she did not receive through gameplay, she found through proximity.

Connection formed in the margins. Relationships built themselves in the hours after the vote, in the shared language that only exists between people who have stepped into something unfamiliar together. Those relationships did not fade with time. They deepened. Through watch parties. Through the long stretch of online games during COVID. Through conversations that extended beyond any single experience.

Years later, many of those people are now woven through the tapestry of Melanie's life. The game ended quickly, but the belonging did not.

Melanie would have it no other way.

Being the first person voted out changes how you understand everything that follows. You do not experience the early formation of trust or the rhythm of strategy unfolding. You experience the edges. The waiting. Perhaps even the quiet question of whether you still matter once the game continues without you.

Melanie carried that perspective with her.

She had come to understand, in a way that cannot be theorized, that one-day games place particular pressure on those early moments. "I need more time to connect with people," she told me simply. The format compresses everything, leaving little room for the kind of trust that builds through proximity and shared endurance.

It shaped the way she thought about the structure of games, about redemption twists, about how early exits are treated by production. She understood that being voted out is not the same as being erased. A game can end for someone and still hold them. It can still honor their presence, still allow them to belong even after their role has shifted.

That belief did not remain abstract.

It became part of how she moved through this community.

When she stepped into production roles, something shifted in her orientation toward the work. "When I'm doing production," she said, "I have a mindset of I'm giving a gift to these other people to have and experience what I've done already." Care, for Melanie, is not incidental to the work. It is the work.

Years later, Melanie arrived at another game and felt something familiar, though this time it unsettled her. She looked around and saw too many of the same faces, too much overlap, too narrow a circle. Nothing was overtly wrong. Nothing was intentionally exclusionary. The community was not broken... but it was closed in a way that had never been examined.

She recognized the pattern immediately. "I was coming to games where I would show up and I would look around and see that all the other players were people that I recognized from past games," she explained. If the same people continued to apply, the same people would continue to be cast. If the same networks remained the primary points of entry, the circle would never widen. Access would continue to be limited, not by design, but by habit.

She understood what that meant. Fewer people would find their way in. Fewer people would experience what she had found, especially those who did not already see themselves reflected in the space.

That is where she noticed the gap.

Not in intention...

In access.

The casting page did not come from a desire to organize or streamline. It came from conviction. Communities do not grow by accident. They expand because someone chooses to widen the doorway. Melanie understood that diverse casts do not begin at casting. They begin much earlier. They begin with awareness. With invitation. With the quiet but powerful question of who even knows these games exist.

Expanding the applicant pool was never about numbers.

It was about equity.

She had looked at the numbers and felt the weight of what they revealed. "For every 85 applications an LRG gets," she said, "85 will be men and maybe 15 women." She traced the reasons carefully, the unequal distribution of caregiving responsibilities, the financial barriers, the gap in confidence that comes from never seeing someone like you take that kind of risk. She understood that closing those gaps required more than open applications. It *required active invitation.*

More applicants creates more possibility. More possibility allows for more representation across race, gender, age, background, and experience. Representation, in turn, strengthens the community itself. It creates a space where more people can enter and recognize that there is room for them, even if they have never seen themselves reflected there before.

For Melanie, this was not theoretical.

It was personal.

She had lived the difference between being included and being overlooked. She had experienced what it meant to be removed from the game and still held by the community that surrounded it. She understood, on a lived level, that belonging does not have to end when the game does.

Melanie does not use the word community casually. She understands it as something necessary, something that holds people together in ways that extend beyond any single experience. It connects people who are similar and people who are not. It creates shared understanding where there was once distance. It expands empathy, not through theory, but through proximity.

What she does might look like coordination from the outside. It might look like outreach or infrastructure. But Melanie's vision of what this space could become is straightforward: "Invite in, everyone come in. Let's grow and compete within the game, but not as games." The community does not benefit from competition between itself. It benefits from expansion.

Melanie is specific about what that expansion requires. "Casting decisions need to be mindful about who they're casting," she pressed. Not in the sense of checking boxes, but in the deeper sense of making diversity a structural priority rather than an afterthought. It must be built into the foundation, not added once growth has already occurred.

At its core, *it is care.* She is not building visibility for herself. She is building connection for others.

My Lens Reframed

Melanie added a powerful layer of depth to how I understand belonging.

It does not always begin at the center. It can take root in the margins... in the spaces where people choose to be even when they are no longer required to. Staying... continuing to participate... becomes its own kind of courage. A decision to keep investing... to stay connected... even when the role itself has shifted.

And that reframes how community is built.

Inclusion is not something added once a space has already taken shape. It lives in the foundation... in the early decisions that determine who feels invited to arrive... and who is able to remain. It is carried in what is encouraged... what is made possible... what is allowed to continue.

And it changes how endings are understood.

An early exit does not have to mean disconnection. A game does not have to continue for belonging to do the same. What is created can extend beyond the moment... if someone chooses to widen the circle... and hold it open.

Because belonging is not defined by where you stand within a structure...

It is defined by the connection that remains... even after your place within it has changed.

WORDS OF WISDOM

"I kept stepping in... because someone needed to."

~ Melanie Bartlett

Voices echo long after the moment has passed.
Decisions stay with us,
shaping how we move forward.
Even the missteps…
especially the missteps…
leave behind something worth holding onto.
No one leaves unchanged,
because of the people who stood beside them
when it mattered most.

Part Five

Beyond the Game

What begins in the woods does not stay there. The lessons ripple outward — into leadership, scholarship, advocacy, family, and future seasons yet to be built. The game becomes a mirror for the larger world, revealing both its fractures and its possibilities. Belonging, once experienced deeply, refuses to stay small. It expands. It evolves. It demands responsibility.

"Structure shapes outcomes."

~ Erin Kunz

Stephen Stewart

Player • LRG Podcaster
• LRG Historian

2024

"I hope whatever you create shows people... this is something they can do too."

Some names do not enter your story only once. They circle you, returning again and again until you realize they have been part of the landscape longer than you understood. Stephen Stewart was one of those names.

The first time I heard it, it was from John (Vataha). Near the end of our interview, almost as an afterthought, he said, *you really need to talk to Stephen.* I scribbled his name on one of the many small pieces of paper that littered my desk during this project, the kind that get folded into books, tucked into coat pockets, and rediscovered weeks later like clues. Then Melanie (Bartlett) said it too. She mentioned a spreadsheet, a timeline, and a kind of documentation that sounded less like a hobby and more like stewardship. When two people point toward the same person independently, you pay attention.

Then came the quiet irony. I realized I had already encountered Stephen before I knew his name. I had seen him in clips, heard references in conversations, noticed him in shared spaces. The community overlaps like Venn diagrams drawn too closely together. You think you are discovering something new, only to realize the story has been orbiting you for years.

When Stephen and I finally spoke, I noticed something steady about him. He wasn't flashy... quite down-to-earth, in fact. His sentences landed with the precision of footnotes, intentional, grounded, and exact.

♦

Stephen does not talk about history like it is trivia. He talks about it like foundation.

He has been quietly building a timeline of Live Reality Games, tracing when series began, when they evolved, when they disappeared. He has tracked *YouTube* uploads from a decade ago and archived seasons that now exist only in half-lit thumbnails and comment sections from years past.

"Pre-2010s, it's going to be pretty murky," he told me, "but a lot of the games we know today, a lot of the big ones, started in the early 2010s."

Before social media began stitching distant hosts together, people were gathering in parks, cabins, and borrowed backyards because they had watched strangers on CBS build shelter and thought, *we could do that*. Those early games were rarely documented with care. They were ephemeral. They existed for a weekend, for a friend group, for a moment that lived mostly in memory.

"If a game doesn't have something on *YouTube*," Stephen said quietly, "there's just no way to know."

He describes a slow and almost accidental discovery... a game host realizing they were not alone, that others had been running the same kind of game in a different state, a different city, with different people who never knew anyone else was doing the same thing.

What Stephen understands instinctively is that communities that do not record themselves eventually forget they existed. He pays attention to that. He believes the timeline becomes clearer in the early 2010s, when YouTube uploads became searchable and social media began stitching distant hosts together. That was when something shifted.

He does not describe that shift with grandiosity. He describes it like someone mapping roots underground. For him, it was never only about dates. It was about belonging.

Stephen is an assistant professor at Trinity University in San Antonio, where he teaches accounting. I had to sit with that for a moment. The man cataloging the history of a movement built on spontaneous, communal, emotionally driven games... teaches accounting.

"I say I'm a glorified algebra teacher," he told me with a slight smile, "because at the end of the day, we're solving for X."

What struck me beyond his delightfully, subtle humor was the through-line. Accounting is about structure, about invisible frameworks that hold visible outcomes together. So is history. So are Live Reality Games. You cannot understand a community unless you understand the systems shaping it.

Stephen sees both, the emotion and the architecture. He understands that the feeling of belonging requires a framework to exist inside. Without that framework, belonging has nowhere to land. It cannot accumulate. It cannot be passed forward.

He is building that framework one entry at a time.

Stephen's first live game was *Pirate Survival Expedition* in 2017. Seven days. Blood vs. Water. Twenty four players. A season that has not run since.

"I came in second," he said. "It was what I called my Survivor Dream and Nightmare combined. I got to the end and just completely —I was not in a good mental place by the game. It was really rough mentally on me."

He does not romanticize the experience. He does not reach for language that makes it something it was not. He remembers the ache of never fully sleeping, the way paranoia seeped into conversation slowly, like condensation on glass.

The deeper you go, the more the game asks of you, he explained. Hunger makes everything louder. Social nuance becomes amplified. Your mind runs constantly, calculating trust, loyalty, risk, and perception. By the time you reach the final days, exhaustion is no longer only physical. It becomes cognitive and emotional as well.

Sometimes making it far does not mean you were okay. Sometimes it means you lasted long enough to see exactly where your limits are and had to keep going anyway.

That honesty is part of what makes Stephen essential to this community. He respects the game, but he does not mythologize it.

◆

During the pandemic, when the world shrank into screens and silence, Stephen joined what became the *Live Reality Game Podcast* alongside Kirk Carlson, Dustin Napper, and Naomi Calhoun.

It began the way so many things in this community begin. Someone asked why not, and everyone else decided to find out.

"I realized, *oh, this is kind of fun,*" Stephen said of those early episodes. "I enjoy talking and pontificating, armchair quarterbacking."

But what the podcast revealed was something beyond commentary. It revealed what Stephen truly cares about. He had already been doing extensive post-game interviews for *Surviving Reelfoot,* and he found himself drawn less to the moves themselves than to what they meant. He cared about what happened after the torch was snuffed. He cared about what happened when someone flew across the country, got voted out early, and still had days left in a place they did not know.

He cared about the moment when adrenaline crashed and a player was left alone with the story they were telling themselves about what had just happened.

"I found the *Bloomington* redemption experience surprisingly more cathartic and enjoyable than I expected it to be," he admitted, describing how live games can extend participation beyond elimination in ways that feel meaningful rather than mechanical.

Stephen listens in the aftermath, in the unedited debrief, in the long conversations that happen after strategy has already done its damage. That is not mere commentary. That is stewardship.

♦

When we spoke about growth in the community, Stephen named something delicate and real.

These games are intimate ecosystems, and the same players often appear across multiple series. Relationships overlap. Friendships predate casting. It creates layered gameplay, but it also creates tension.

"Those two weren't actually strangers," he said, describing the experience of a first-time player arriving with full enthusiasm into a cast where others already had history. "You have people who are just like, wait—I'm here to play *Survivor*. Sixteen strangers. And then you realize —" he paused. "That's not quite what this is."

He does not condemn either approach. He frames it as evolution, as a growing pain within a community that is still trying to understand itself. For him, the greater concern is accessibility.

He told me about the day he dragged his middle brother to a one-day Blood vs. Water game in Los Angeles.

"Steve, I'm only doing this because of you," his brother told him at the start.

His brother ended up winning.

"I think you're still insane for doing this," the brother admitted after it was over, "but this was more fun than I thought it would be."

That story lives in a drawer Stephen returns to often. Because the worst outcome is not simply losing. The worst outcome is someone leaving early and deciding never to return.

"The worst thing that could possibly happen," he said, "is someone comes out, does it, they've never done it before, they're the first boot— and they're like, yep. Never again."

That sentence is a design principle. It is a philosophy. It is an argument for why craft matters. Stephen sees Live Reality Games as part of *Survivor's* extended legacy, not imitation but continuation. He sees them as a living echo, an experiment that outgrew its source.

He hopes whatever story gets told about this community functions as what he called *a love letter*. Welcoming. Opening. Honest about the difficulty while still making room for the newcomer who is standing at the edge of the woods, wondering whether they belong.

They do... and Stephen wants them to know that.

MY LENS REFRAMED

Stephen reminded me that passion without documentation risks being forgotten.

A community can feel vibrant and alive... and still disappear if no one records its roots. Memory anchors meaning. Without it, stories begin to drift... details soften... and what once felt whole becomes fragmented over time.

He reframed history for me... not as nostalgia, but as responsibility.

Because what feels alive in one moment can fade in the next... unless someone chooses to remember it with intention. Documentation becomes more than record. It becomes preservation... a way of anchoring meaning so it does not slip away... a way of ensuring that what was built is not lost to time, and that the people who shaped it are not reduced to fragments or forgotten entirely.

And there is something else that emerges when that work is done well.

A deeper sense of belonging.

When history is visible... people can see themselves not as isolated participants, but as part of something that existed before them... and will continue after them. A timeline begins to take shape... one that holds not just events, but presence... connection... continuity.

And what stays with me is this...

What is remembered does not disappear.

It lives on... held in place by someone who understood that it was worth keeping.

ANGELA L. MILLER

PLAYER • VOLUNTEER

2026

"I want them to think... damn, she has a life well lived."

The Louisville sun filled the room with a steady, generous light. We had only just arranged the call when she agreed to jump on, no time to prepare or shift anything around her. She was sitting in a chair in what looked like her living room, her royal blue sweater giving the softest hint of a cozy Sunday afternoon. There was something unguarded about the moment... as though nothing needed to be adjusted for her to simply be herself.

She answered questions the way some people arrange flowers... carefully, attentively, with a clear sense that beauty and truth deserve time. "I feel like I need to start at the beginning," she said... and she meant it.

Nothing in Angela rushed. Even when I tried to move us forward, she would return, gently but firmly, to finish the thought she had begun. There was no tension in it, no disruption to the conversation, only a quiet commitment to completing what mattered. I found myself adjusting to her pace without realizing it, listening more closely, allowing space to exist where I might normally move ahead. It is revealing the way a person chooses to answer a question. Angela does not reach for efficiency... she reaches for accuracy, and in doing so, she reveals what she values.

There is a softness to her that draws you in before you have the chance to understand her. She is small in frame, with large expressive eyes and a gorgeous smile that gives her a kind of agelessness, as though time has not settled on her in the way it does for others. There is a kindness in her presence that feels immediate and unguarded. It would be easy to stop there in your understanding of her, to let that be the full picture.

As she spoke, it became clear that what is visible is only the surface of something far more considered. Angela carries a life that has required her to make difficult choices, to navigate loss, to adapt, to return to herself again and again. There is an intentionality in her that does not announce itself, but it is there in the way she speaks, in the way she reflects, in the way she does not rush past what deserves to be understood. She knows herself in a way that feels lived in... not something she arrived at quickly, but something she has come to over time, through experience that asked something of her.

She came into this world of games through love. Long before she ever stepped into one, she had been watching *Survivor*, paying attention to what it required of people. She understood something early that many come to later... that the game is built on perception, timing, and the ability to read what is happening beneath what is being said. There is a kind of listening required for that, and Angela already knew how to listen.

When she applied to *Survival Challenge*, it came together quickly, almost unexpectedly. "What's the worst thing that can happen?"

Then came the call, and with it, the realization that she would need to meet the opportunity with preparation. Angela responded in the way she tends to... with thoughtfulness and follow through. She taught herself how to swim. She walked for miles. She practiced balance challenges in her home, using what she had around her, turning ordinary objects into something purposeful. She studied. She imagined.

She prepared in a way that reflected not only her desire to play, but her willingness to take the experience seriously.

As she continued telling her story, the shape of it began to expand beyond the game itself. The preparation, the decision to show up, the changes she was making... they were not isolated. They were part of something happening in her life at the same time.

Angela had been estranged from her daughter, a separation shaped by addiction, pain, and the kind of love that sometimes requires distance in order to remain intact. She spoke about it plainly, without trying to reshape it into something easier to hold. There are moments in life where love requires a different kind of expression, one that does not always look like closeness.

As she began making changes in her life to prepare for the game, something shifted. Her daughter noticed, "And it helped us reconnect," Angela shares.

There are moments in these conversations where I feel the need to pause, not to respond, but to take in what has just been said. This was one of them. "It would not have happened if it weren't for *Survival Challenge*."

The meaning of that does not sit on the surface. It asks for a different kind of attention. It suggests that something we might be tempted to dismiss can become something far more significant in the context of a person's life.

Angela entered her first LRG with an awareness of how she might be perceived. She understood the gap between how she experiences herself and how others might interpret her presence.

"That's what they see... but I don't see myself that way—I don't feel like my current age is 52."

She does not resist that difference. She observes it. She understands that generational language, humor, and shared experience create immediate connection for some and distance for others. She knows that she may not be immediately placed within the same frame as the people around her. And still, she engages.

◆

There was another layer to Angela's experience that I understood immediately because, in different ways, we both live inside it. We are both hard of hearing. The specifics are different, but the constant negotiation of sound, conversation, space, and exhaustion felt deeply familiar to me as she spoke.

At one point in the interview, I laughed and told her about a recent game where I had finally brought my hearing aid with me, convinced it was going to solve everything. Instead, I spent half the game frustrated because I still could not hear instructions clearly. One challenge completely unraveled for me because I missed that a transition had already happened. By the end of the week, I remember thinking...*I can't do this anymore.*

Angela understood instantly. There was no need to over explain it.

"When people whisper, I hear the sound...but I don't understand the words."

The two of us laughed at that in the way people do when something is both funny and exhausting at the same time. Anyone outside of these games might underestimate how much whispering happens inside an LRG. Entire alliances can form in half sentences spoken while walking past each other. Information moves quickly, quietly, constantly. Sometimes everyone around you seems to know something a full ten minutes before you do.

Angela described sitting at Tribal Council during her first game while people directly behind her whispered back and forth. She knew conversations were happening. She could hear the rhythm of speech, the movement of voices, the hush of strategy unfolding inches away from her... but not the actual words themselves.

"I've always had a problem with whispers."

I understood that immediately. There is a very specific frustration in hearing enough to know you are missing information, but not enough to actually access it. It creates a strange kind of separation where you are fully present and still partially outside the moment.

Angela also lives with Meniere's disease, which affects hearing, balance, and orientation. She described episodes of vertigo so severe the room would spin violently around her. Listening to her speak, I found myself thinking about how much invisible adaptation exists underneath

participation for people navigating disabilities that others cannot
always see.

And still...she plays.

She adjusts. She studies environments differently. She pays attention
to movement, body language, emotional shifts, tone, pacing. Listening,
for Angela, extends far beyond sound alone.

What I admired most was the complete absence of self pity in the
way she spoke about any of it. There was honesty, frustration at times,
humor even...but never self pity. She approached it the same way she
seemed to approach most things in her life...as something real to
navigate rather than something requiring performance or explanation.

At one point she talked about finally getting newer hearing aids that
allowed her to better adjust sound outdoors during games. There was
genuine excitement in her voice describing the difference it made. I
smiled listening to her because there is something profoundly bonding
about two people who understand exactly how triumphant it can feel to
simply hear the instructions correctly.

People often saw Angela's age first. Some likely saw softness first.
Some underestimated her entirely. What they did not immediately see
was the extraordinary amount of interpretation happening beneath the
surface the entire time... balancing physical symptoms, processing
fragmented sound, reading emotion, observing patterns, and remaining
socially engaged all at once.

There is a quiet fierceness in that kind of adaptation. The kind built
slowly through lived experience. The kind that does not ask for
attention because it has already become part of how a person survives,
connects, and moves through the world.

Over time, she has built connections that extend beyond those
initial perceptions. Relationships that are grounded in something
deeper than age or familiarity. There is an openness in her that allows
that to happen, a willingness to meet people where they are without
needing to resolve the differences first.

As the conversation continued, something else began to take shape.

It revealed itself at an organic pace. It was not stated directly, rather it emerged in the way she talked about emotional investment, in the way she described her experiences inside the game.

"It's because we're emotionally invested... because it matters," Angela explained. "When I go in with no expectations... I have fun. When I have expectations... that's what does me in."

There was a steadiness in the way she said it, as though she had come to understand something about herself that she could now name clearly. It was somewhere in that part of the conversation that I felt the shift. Not in her tone, but in what was being revealed underneath her words.

She was not only describing how she plays. She was describing the cost of staying deeply invested. "If you're still reeling from the pain a week later... you probably shouldn't be playing."

I let that sit for a moment before I responded. It felt like one of those places where the conversation could easily move on... or it could be held a little longer.

So I asked her, not as a formal question, but as something I was trying to understand myself... *How do we know when it is time to step away... or take a break... or make the decision not to play at all?*

Angela did not rush her answer. She never does. She spoke about emotional exhaustion, about the way experiences inside the game can connect to parts of life that exist far beyond it. She spoke about the way disappointment can linger, not because something went wrong, but because something mattered. She spoke about paying attention to what happens after... to how long something stays with you, to what it begins to take from you if you are not careful.

She did not simplify what she had experienced. She allowed it to remain layered, to hold more than one truth at once.

She understands that people can be kind and still leave you feeling unseen. That a community can hold meaning and still bring moments of discomfort. That something can be both life giving and, at times, difficult to carry. That kind of awareness does not come quickly. It is something she has come to through experience, through reflection, through allowing herself to be honest about what she feels.

And still, she holds onto what is meaningful within it. "It takes a certain kind of person... to want to go out and be vulnerable." She knows that kind of person well... because she has chosen to be one.

There is a creativity woven through the way Angela moves through the world. She writes music. She thinks in rhythm. She notices detail, whether in how something looks, how it feels, or how it is built. That same attention shows up in the way she participates in this community. When she cannot play, she finds another way to stay connected. "If I can't win... I want to volunteer."

There is something revealing in that instinct. It speaks to the way she values the experience beyond outcome. It also offers another way of understanding what it means to step back... that it does not always require leaving entirely, but sometimes invites a different kind of presence.

When I asked her what she hoped people would take away from her story, her answer came without hesitation. "I want them to think... damn, she has a life well lived."

There is something grounding in that. A life measured not by ease or certainty, but by participation, by willingness, by the decision to show up even when the outcome is unknown.

Listening to Angela, it is clear that she has shown up for her life in ways that have asked something of her, and she has continued to return to herself in the process.

My Lens Reframed

Angela reshaped the way I think about participation itself... about what it quietly asks of people whose abilities require constant adaptation in spaces that were not necessarily designed with them in mind. Listening to her, I kept thinking about how much energy can go into simply staying connected to the moment... hearing enough, catching enough, processing enough, remaining socially present while information moves quickly around you.

It also made me wonder how many others might step into these spaces if conversations like this were spoken more openly... if there were greater recognition of the different ways people experience these games and the invisible work some players are doing simply to remain part of them.

Angela also changed where my attention goes.

I had often thought about these experiences in terms of what happens inside them... the strategy, the outcome, the moments that are visible to others. She drew my attention somewhere else entirely... to what happens after... to the weight of emotional investment.

The impact is not only what happened, but how much it mattered while you were inside of it. Memory is tied to care... and with care, there is weight. And that weight asks something of us.

It asks us to notice what lingers... to recognize when something begins to take more than it gives... to listen for the quiet moment when something inside us begins to ask a different question.

And that awareness carries its own kind of discernment.

To recognize what is life-giving... and when something begins to ask more than it should. To understand that disappointment can remain... not because something went wrong, but because something mattered. To pay attention to what comes after... and to allow that to shape what we choose next.

And still... connection does not have to end.

Stepping back does not always mean leaving. Sometimes it looks like choosing a different way to remain... to contribute... to support... to stay connected without carrying the same weight.

There is a fullness in the way she moves through her life... a willingness to participate... to stay open... to keep returning even when the experience is not simple.

A life not measured by ease... but by presence.

"I want them to think... damn, she has a life well lived." And listening to her... you understand that she does.

Danny Vogwill

Player • Creator • Volunteer

2024

"We're forming something real with people we would never meet… and somehow, it still matters."

Some people walk into a room and immediately take up space. Their presence is felt through volume, through movement, through an unmistakable shift in attention that pulls everything toward them. You know they have arrived because the energy reorganizes itself around their voice, their posture, and their need to be seen. Danny enters a room and something else happens entirely. The space does not tighten or redirect. It settles. It exhales. It becomes, almost imperceptibly at first, more livable.

More joyful.

I noticed it before I understood it. There was a pause where there usually would have been interruption, the kind of pause that does not signal awkwardness, but permission. Conversations slowed without losing their substance. Shoulders lowered as if something unspoken had been set down. Voices softened, not out of caution, but out of ease. No one mentioned the shift, and yet everyone lived in it. Danny has no need to claim rooms. They were precise in who they were, and that precision created a kind of safety that did not need explanation.

Before I had language for what Danny was doing, I watched. I watched how people adjusted in their presence, not because they were told to, but because something about the environment invited a different kind of being. Conflict did not disappear, but it changed shape. Disagreement ensued, but it did not escalate into something sharper or more defensive.

People were allowed to be imperfect without being reduced to that imperfection.

Danny was not directing... they were stabilizing, holding in a way that makes it possible for others to stay present inside themselves.

There is a kind of power that creates conditions where honesty can exist without fear of immediate consequence. Not everything that supports a structure is visible, and yet the strength of that structure depends entirely on what cannot be seen at first glance.

Danny wields that kind of power. They embody it in a way that feels both intentional and effortless, though it is neither simple nor accidental.

♦

Danny understands something that many people spend years trying to articulate. Being visible is not the same as being known. Visibility can be imposed. It can be demanded, distorted, or granted in ways that have very little to do with authenticity.

Knowing requires something slower, something built over time through consistency and trust. In a space that rewards exposure, where cunning moves and emphatic voices often define the narrative, Danny resists the urge to make themselves easily legible. They allow themselves to be seen without surrendering authorship of their own story. They do not offer pieces of themselves for quick interpretation, and they do not hide either. They trust the process of being seen first and then known, even when that process moves slower than the environment may reward.

♦

When Danny describes first stepping into a live game as a player—
their first time, years of hosting behind them and still not quite knowing
what they would find on the other side—the language that comes is not
one of strategy or preparation. *It is wonder.*

"It was honestly insane," they said. "It was everything I had hoped it
was going to be. I had never camped like that before. I didn't know any
of those people, and to this day one of my best friends is from that
game."

Danny's enthusiasm and awe are felt as they spoke. The recognition
of something genuinely discovered—that what Danny had spent years
building for others, they had finally stepped inside themselves. The
game gave them what it gives many people who walk into it without
quite knowing why: the experience of being present with strangers in a
way that leaves no room for distance.

The moments that revealed Danny most clearly were often the
smallest. They did not live in theatrical gestures or defining speeches.
They lived in the way Danny handled language. When pronouns were
misused, Danny corrected them with a calm that did not invite
discomfort or apology. The correction was clear, direct, and complete. It
did not linger. It did not expand into something heavier than it needed
to be. It simply reestablished truth and moved forward. Watching that
happen repeatedly revealed how often clarity is softened to make it
easier for others to receive, and how rare it is for someone to refuse that
expectation without becoming hardened. Danny did not ask to be
accommodated. They insisted on being accurate, and they did so
without turning accuracy into confrontation.

Language, in Danny's presence, became something steadier. Words
were not used to dominate or to perform intelligence. They were chosen
carefully, offered with intention, and grounded in care. In a space where
speech often becomes strategy, Danny created something different.

They made language feel like a place people could stand without
preparing to defend themselves. They listened more than they spoke,
and when they did speak, their words carried weight because they were

precise. Even during our interview, Danny kept returning to people with a grace that felt hard won. "I don't know what's going on in peoples' lives," they said... and that awareness seemed to shape not only how they played, but how they moved through the world.

"People are more vulnerable and share more about themselves because we are not in their everyday life," Danny told me. "So people feel more open to share things about themselves with players, and that's super cathartic... You have so much to share and I have so much to say, so let's fill each other in."

That is not an observation made from outside the experience. It is something Danny has lived. In the compression of a multi-day game, stripped of phones and ordinary life, something else fills the space. Trust forms quickly because the conditions remove the usual reasons for withholding it.

◆

What Danny offers comes at a cost. Restraint is often misunderstood. It is easy to mistake it for passivity or distance, to assume that what is not asserted or demanding of center stage is somehow less present. In environments that reward performance, the refusal to over-perform can make someone less visible within the narrative that others are constructing. Danny did not posture or exaggerate to claim space within that narrative. They did not chase validation or reshape themselves to become more easily understood. As a result, they were not always centered in the way brassy forms of leadership often are. Quiet integrity rarely is.

Danny recalled playing a game that did not reward the kind of leadership they embodied. There was no visible resentment, no attempt to become something more palatable or more easily recognized. Danny chose to remain consistent in who they were, even when consistency did not translate into advantage. That is a form of courage that is rarely discussed, because it does not draw attention to itself. It simply exists, rooted and unchanging.

There was something similar in the way they spoke about growth. Danny described his experiences as places that reveal. Places where confidence is built, where people surprise themselves, where even the hard lessons matter. "I need to back myself some more," they said, reflecting on what these spaces had taught them. In another voice, the line might have sounded small. In Danny's, it felt honest and earned.

Part of what has shaped that reflection is how Danny has learned to remember an experience after it ends. Not to let it collapse under its own weight, but to shape it with wisdom.

"Sometimes I'll write down fun things that happened during the game instead of dwelling on the negative parts," they said. "I'll forget the positive moments if I just dwell on the bad ones."

That is not avoidance. It is curation. The willingness to hold a complicated experience with both hands, keeping what is worth keeping, without letting the difficult parts crowd out what deserves to part of the experience and remembered.

The moment that has stayed with me most is one Danny described from their very first long-form game. It was late. Night four or five. The finale was in sight. Danny and their closest ally had found something like rhythm, a rare thing inside a game built on disruption. And then, in a small moment between two people, something unexpected happened.

"He looked at me and he goes, Danny, I've never had any other queer friends. You're my first queer friend. That just means so much to me." Danny's voice quieted. "I literally just started crying. I would be nowhere without my queer friends. I remember how lonely it was in elementary school without that. So I was like—if I can be that for him... I've won."

No phone. No internet. No ordinary life to retreat into. Just a night in the Canadian wilderness and a confession that could only have arrived in that exact space, at that exact time, with that exact degree of openness. "Literally no phones, no connecting with people," Danny said afterward, almost laughing at the speed of it. "And then guess what? I went right back to game mode."

That is what Danny means when they say we are forming something real. Not the game itself, but what the game makes possible. The conversation that would not have happened elsewhere. The connection that forms... not in spite of the pressure, but because of it.

◆

I noticed a pattern with Danny... Danny did not translate themselves for others. They did not dilute their identity to make it more comfortable for someone else to understand. They did not over-explain their humanity or perform accessibility. They trusted that the right people would meet them where they stood, and that those who did not were not owed a version of them that felt easier to receive. That kind of trust is not passive. It is a decision made repeatedly, often in moments where the easier choice would be to adapt.

"The concept of *Survivor*," Danny said, "of forming a new society with people while battling the elements—that's really poetic. Because that's kind of what you do in these LRGs. And it's a time for people to meet and connect with other people that—even when you may not have any common ground with them—you can always talk about the game that you're competing in."

When our interview was over, I sat back and smiled. I returned to the way the room changed when they entered it. I thought about the way people breathed differently, spoke differently, existed differently without fully realizing why... and I thought about what it means to hold space without needing to own it.

My Lens Reframed

Danny changed how I understand leadership in a way I did not expect.

I am used to noticing what is said... what is done... what is claimed. Being with them drew my attention somewhere quieter... to what is held. To the way a space is carried... the way presence itself can shape what happens within it.

What I saw is that safety is not softness... and it is not passive.

It is a disciplined practice of presence. A commitment to how you show up... moment by moment... in the choices you make with and for other people. It is choosing directness over comfort... consistency over performance... integrity over recognition.

And what I witnessed was not quietness.

It was precision.

The kind that does not announce itself... but is felt in how a space begins to respond. In how people settle... in how they speak... in what becomes possible when they no longer have to brace.

Safety is not something we declare.

It is something we build... through the accumulation of choices... through the willingness to remain attentive... through the discipline it takes to hold a space without needing to control it.

There is a difference between being seen and being known.

And there is a quiet authority in choosing the pace at which you allow yourself to be understood... not as withdrawal... but as discernment. As a way of remaining grounded in who you are without performing for recognition.

Integrity does not need amplification.

It reveals itself in what holds.

In the moments where correction does not wound... where honesty does not require force... where presence alone begins to change the room.

And often... though it may go unnamed... everything is somehow different.

Erin O'Mara Kunz

Player • Social Psychologist

2026

"Anything that makes you different... you feel it."

"Why do I love something that doesn't love me back?" She didn't say it lightly. It came after another game. Another near miss. Another moment where she had shown up prepared, thoughtful, strategic — and still found herself outside the merge, outside the circle, outside the table.

She was home. Talking to her husband. Crying. It was "just a game,"... but the feeling wasn't new. There is something uniquely disorienting about repeatedly entering a space you deeply love — and being told, in subtle or direct ways, that you don't quite fit."

It was not only another loss. It was the repetition of it. Another pre merge exit. Another moment of arriving prepared, thoughtful, and strategic, only to find herself outside the circle. Outside the vote. Outside the invisible boundary where belonging is granted.

Erin is a social psychologist who studies bias, group dynamics, and identity. She understands structural inequity in theory. It feels entirely different when your own name is written down.

She almost did not play *Survivor Indiana* in the summer of 2025.

She considered telling herself that she was too busy, too established, too far along in her life to continue stepping into environments that did not seem built with her in mind. It would have been easy to remove herself before anyone else could.

Instead, she completed the application. That decision was quiet and unceremonious, but it marked the point where her story shifted.

Erin has never loved *Survivor* casually. She was in college when Richard Hatch won, sitting in a dorm suite with twenty friends, the air filled with the scent of microwaved popcorn and carpet cleaner. While others were focused on the visible elements of the game, the fire, the shelter, the competition, Erin was drawn to something else entirely. She watched the dynamics between people.

She wondered how someone could betray another person and still receive their vote. She wondered how trust could fracture and still be rebuilt in the same space. Even then, before graduate school and research and teaching, her attention was already tuned toward power, perception, and belonging.

Years later, when she began to see patterns in early eliminations, she did not comment casually. She built a dataset. She analyzed seasons one through forty, tracking who left first, who left before the merge, who reached the final, and who won. The patterns emerged quickly. Women and people of color were disproportionately eliminated early. Women of color most of all. The effect was strongest in early phases of the game, when belonging is fragile and collective, and it lessened as the game shifted toward individual agency.

Structure shapes outcome.

It is one thing to publish that conclusion. It is another to carry it into the woods.

Her first live game was *Survival Challenge*. There were three players over forty in a cast of twenty five, and four parents. Tribes of five leave little room for difference to soften. Every deviation is amplified. Every distinction becomes a label.

No one needed to say she was older. The implication was already present.

The tribe lost. Stress rose quickly. Feedback shifted in tone. Words that might seem neutral on the surface carried familiar undertones. She was described as intense. As not handling it well. As strategic. The language echoed experiences she had encountered before, both in research and in life.

Her family had traveled to watch. Her mother was in the audience. After her torch was extinguished, Erin glanced in that direction, the smell of smoke still lingering, the emotion in her eyes not entirely caused by the flame.

She was the first voted out.

It is striking how quickly early experiences can return in an adult body. The feeling of standing slightly apart. The effort to appear unaffected. The reality of caring deeply anyway.

Even after she would go on to win another game, that first elimination stayed with her. It was never only about gameplay. It was about belonging.

Still, she did not withdraw.

At *Survivor Indiana*, the summer air was thick, pressing against the skin, the ground damp in the early morning. During the *Will It Go Round* challenge, the mechanism did not work at first. The structure resisted her hands. Tyler (Allen) began counting down. His voice felt louder than it likely was, each number landing with weight.

Then something shifted. The mechanism began to move. The motion steadied.

At that moment, the challenge was no longer about another competitor. It became internal. It became a confrontation with the part of herself that had learned to step back early.

Her arms began to ache, not dramatically, but steadily. Her back tightened. Her breath shortened. Her mind offered her an exit, a familiar thought that she had already done enough.

She moved past the initial discomfort and into the deeper strain, the point where muscles begin to shake and the body demands relief. The world narrowed to repetition. Motion continued. Breath continued.

When she finally stepped down, she had set a record.

Erin would win three individual immunities, but the most significant shift had already occurred. She did not leave first.

Winning carries its own consequences. Visibility creates risk. Earlier versions of Erin might have minimized that attention, softened her presence, or apologized for standing out.

This version did not.

She spoke clearly. She acted with intention. She balanced kindness with directness. She no longer reduced herself to make others comfortable. She allowed her different roles to exist together rather than choosing between them.

Winning immunities can paint a target, but Erin had learned something from her earlier losses. Play with your head, not just your heart.

Assume nothing. Say the thing. Be direct.

She learned that kindness and strategy are not opposites. She learned that clarity does not equal cruelty. She learned that being older does not require shrinking. She integrated. The scientist and the competitor. The heart and the head. The resilience and the softness. She didn't perform youth. She didn't minimize her experience. She didn't apologize for taking up space.

Instead, Erin won.

♦

Near the end of our conversation, something happened that revealed even more than the game. Her child appeared, needing attention in a moment that could not be postponed. Without hesitation, Erin shifted. She poured cereal, negotiated small preferences, and adjusted to the needs in front of her.

Her voice softened, but her clarity did not change. There was no apology for the interruption. There was no attempt to separate these parts of her life. When she returned to our conversation, she resumed her thought seamlessly, continuing her analysis without losing precision.

The game measures physical endurance. It does not measure the ability to shift between roles, to carry responsibility in multiple spaces, or to maintain focus through constant interruption.

Watching her, I understood that her success was not sudden. It was cumulative.

Erin now teaches a course on *Survivor*, exploring bias, group dynamics, identity, and belonging. She is writing a book that connects social psychology with the game, recognizing that *Survivor* is not trivial. It is a condensed form of human behavior.

Her legacy is not only that she won. It is that she refused to remove herself before the game could.

She entered spaces that quietly suggested she did not belong and responded not with spectacle, but with presence.

My Lens Reframed

Erin reshaped how I understand representation.

It is not singular. It is layered. Race, gender, age, and life stage all influence how people are perceived and how they are treated. Even when these differences are unspoken, they do not disappear. They move quietly... shaping perception, influencing decision, determining outcome before they are ever acknowledged.

What stayed with me is how she moved within that.

She did not respond with anger... but with inquiry. With persistence. With a willingness to be present long enough to outlast the assumptions placed on her.

There is always the option to step back... to withdraw before the outcome is decided... to protect yourself from what has already begun to take shape. She does not choose that.

Erin remains.

Bias does not always announce itself. It lives in patterns... in systems... in the quiet ways decisions are made and reinforced over time. But so does something else.

The possibility of staying long enough to challenge what has already been assumed.

Not through force... but through presence. Through persistence. Through a steady refusal to disappear.

And there is something else at work in that space...

A refusal to divide herself in order to be understood.

Not separating intellect from care... or strength from motherhood... or presence from performance... but carrying all of it... fully... into the moment.

A life is not one surface.

It is something more layered... more dimensional... like a gemstone catching light from every angle.

Each facet reveals something different... and none of it diminishes the whole.

There is tension in that space... a quiet decision made again and again to remain... to not reduce what has always existed together.

Erin did not succeed in spite of who she is.

She succeeded because she refused to be anything less.

She succeeded because she refused to fragment herself...

And she won as a whole person.

We may arrive as strangers,
uncertain of what will unfold…
but we leave carrying pieces of one another,
woven quietly into who we are.

Afterword
A Growing Nation

This book did not begin with a manuscript. It began with a moment that refused to leave me.

After playing *Surviving Bloomington* in 2024, I returned home carrying something I could not easily name... but it was powerful. It was not tied to placement or outcome. It wasn't rooted in spectacle or the surface story others might assume. What stayed with me lived underneath all of that... in the spaces between conversations, in the pauses that stretched just a second longer than expected, in the quiet recalibrations happening inside people who had nowhere to hide.

I witnessed courage that did not announce itself. I witnessed insecurity that had no time to mask. I witnessed leadership that emerged without permission, without title, and without introduction. I watched bias rise to the surface before comfort could smooth it over. I watched strangers become reflections, not always gentle ones, but honest ones. Something in me recognized that what I was seeing was not confined to a game. It was human. It was real. It was worth preserving.

The interviews began quickly, almost before I had time to question the instinct. Not to document strategy. Not to dissect gameplay. I was not searching for moves or outcomes. *I was searching for people... I was searching for story because I longed for meaning.* I wanted to understand what happens when the layers fall away, when the noise quiets, and when identity is no longer curated but revealed.

Live Reality Games do not remove reality. They concentrate it.

The phone disappears. Routine dissolves. Distraction fades. What surfaces is a clearer view of who we are when we are seen and when we are stretched. Pressure does not create character. It reveals it. Scarcity does not invent bias. It exposes it. Power does not define instinct. It magnifies what is already present. Exclusion does not begin in the woods. It awakens something that has often been carried long before arrival.

What unfolds in a matter of days in these spaces unfolds across years in our everyday lives. In boardrooms. In classrooms. In families. In communities. The difference is not substance. It is speed. The patterns are the same. The stakes feel different. The mirror is simply closer.

As the conversations deepened, something else began to take shape. Not a conclusion, but a thread that wove its way through every story. Belonging is not passive. It requires courage. Community does not sustain itself. It requires stewardship. Growth does not arrive comfortably. It requires friction. Staying is never automatic. It requires choice.

None of these truths belong only to the woods. They follow us home.

There are many, many voices that live beyond these pages. People who shaped this Nation and early games like *Survivor Angelica*. Builders who carried weight long before recognition arrived. Players whose transformation continues, still unfolding, still becoming. Protectors who chose quiet over visibility, whose impact will never be measured by attention, yet will echo in ways that matter far more.

Their absence here does not diminish their presence in this story. It expands it and calls for more stories to be told. This book is not a conclusion. It is a room with a view. There will be more rooms and alternate views... as there should be.

LRG Nation cannot be contained within chapters or a single book. It exists in the spaces between people, in the choices made when no one is watching, in the willingness to return and try again with more awareness, more care, more intention. It is still growing... and it will continue to grow long after this book is closed.

If something in these pages stirred within you, there is a reason for that. The resonance is not accidental. These stories travel because they are rooted in something universal. You will find yourself in rooms where you are not immediately understood. You will step into spaces that stretch you beyond what feels comfortable. You will encounter moments that press against your edges, revealing what is still unfinished, still tender, still evolving. There will be times when withdrawal feels easier. Times when misunderstanding feels heavy. Times when underestimation tempts you to shrink.

Those moments are not interruptions. They are a call to step into the unknown and meet yourself.

The question will not be whether you are winning. The question will be who you are choosing to become while you are there.

Integrity does not require an audience. Resilience does not require scarcity. Belonging does not require permission. These are not conditions that must be granted. They are choices that can be made. Quietly. Consistently. Wherever you find yourself standing.

Belonging begins when someone chooses to be open instead of retreating. Growth begins when someone chooses to reflect instead of react. Community begins when someone chooses responsibility instead of ego. These choices are seldom loud. They rarely receive recognition. Yet they are the ones that shape everything that follows.

The games come to an end. The fire burns low. The paths clear.

What remains is only what *you* carry forward.

If you close this book feeling inspired, let that be a spark. Let it warm you for a moment. Then let it deepen into something steadier. Inspiration can flicker and it can fade as quickly as it arrives. What endures is something else. Something far more powerful... the belief that you are capable of building what you seek—and the choice to create it.

And this Nation... this living, evolving reflection of humanity at its most honest... will continue to grow in every place those choices are made.

~ *Marya*

Meet the Nation's Contributors

Alicia Garza is the Live-Streamer and Executive Producer of *Can You Survive*. Equally comfortable in front of and behind the camera, she is an aspiring travel influencer who enjoys exploring new locales with her best friend and hopes to inspire other would-be travelers to do the same. A veritable city girl, Alicia is based in New York City but journeys to Maine each year for *Can You Survive*, which she affectionately describes as *adult summer camp*. She loves spending the best week of her year with all the "CYS" alumni who return to volunteer year after year.

Allen Yannone is a proud dad of two boys who keep him constantly on his toes and make life a lot more fun. Most of his favorite moments happen just hanging out with them, whether they're playing, laughing, or getting into a little chaos together. Being their dad is the most important role he has, and he's focused on raising them to be confident, kind, and to always believe in themselves. They are a big part of why he approaches everything in life with energy and purpose.

Creatively, Allen is a Senior Video Producer at MIT, where he tells meaningful stories and brings big ideas to life through video. He has worked across documentaries, branded content, and live productions, and thrives on the challenge of creating work that truly connects with people. He also owns and operates his own video production company, collaborating with clients while continuing to push his creative limits. Storytelling has always been at the center of what he does, both professionally and personally.

In 2020, Allen discovered the world of Live Reality Games, and it immediately clicked for him. He fell in love with the strategy, creativity, and the way it brings people together in a unique, immersive way. That passion grew into something bigger when he and his wife, Kadie Yannone, co-founded *The Reality Retreat.* Together, they built it as a place where anyone can step into their own live reality game experience, with a full team handling production so players can fully dive into the moment. It has been incredibly rewarding for him to create something that blends competition, storytelling, and community.

At his core, everything Allen does comes back to connection. Whether he is behind a camera, building a new experience, or spending time with his family, he is driven to create moments that people remember. He is fueled by creativity, grounded in family, and always looking for the next story to tell.

Alyson Foisy grew up in a small town in Central Massachusetts, and always looked forward to summer camping trips with her family. Performing in musical theatre since childhood provided an endearing sense of self, fueling her creativity. Her search for adventure continued to grow after college, as she moved to NYC, Miami, Orlando, then back up to MA. She worked as a server and brand ambassador at the *Survivor Ultimate Fan Cafe*, in both the Boston and Miami locations!

Alyson lives a thoughtful life full of fun, which transcends into her LRG involvement! Over the past four years, she has played in 10 LRGs, primarily *Survivor* based, across MA, ME, IL, NY, IN, and TN. She volunteers on production for several games, lending support to players and eagerly capturing their storylines behind the camera. She has also stepped into a role as the new host for a game close to her hometown. LRGs have added significant value to her life in means of friendship, personal growth, and exploration. No matter the outcome of a game, Alyson is able to relive the nostalgia of summer camping for which she is grateful.

Amos Ray Smith was born and raised in a small community nestled in the banks of Reelfoot Lake in northwest Tennessee. He has been with his partner for 18 years. In 2021, they were blessed to have the opportunity to grow their family and took in their twin nephews. Amos is active in animal rescue and human rights. He has a creative mind and is always looking for his next big adventure.

In 2014, Amos created *Surviving Reelfoot*, an 8 day *Survivor*-style game. *Surviving Reelfoot* is one of the oldest and longest LRGs in the world. The game has built a community of people from around the world.

Angela L. Miller is an active member of the LRG community, where she has played in multiple games and contributed behind the scenes as a volunteer. She has also competed in online reality games (ORGs), finishing as a runner-up in both formats. Known for her calm, observant approach, Angela tends to play a thoughtful, steady game while others lean into chaos.

Angela is drawn to LRGs for the strategy, connection, and unpredictability they bring, but has come to appreciate just as much what they reveal about people. Her experiences reflect both the beauty of the community and the more complicated realities that can come with high-pressure social gameplay. She is especially interested in how perception shapes reality in these environments, and how those experiences carry over after the game ends.

Angela values authenticity in both gameplay and relationships, and believes you don't have to be the loudest player to have a meaningful impact. Outside of the game, she enjoys spending time with her parents, daughter, sister, brother-in-law, and her beloved dog, Gigi. She lives in Louisville, Kentucky.

Brittany J lives in Indiana. She is a wife, mother and an athlete. When Brittany isn't working or taking care of family, she's training for triathlons, including swimming, biking, running and strength training. While training she needed shows to watch and she became an avid watcher of *Survivor*, *Big Brother*, and *Amazing Race*. She always wondered how she would do on the show *Survivor*. She loves the challenges and the social aspect. Then she discovered the LRG world and applied to Surviving Bloomington to test her skills.

Carlos Kiddo*

Chris Lord is a longtime *Survivor* super-fan from upstate New York. One of his proudest life moments is discovering *Survivor*—and its passionate community—entirely on his own. Through his love of the game, he's built hundreds of friendships online and within the live reality game community. That obsession opened doors, connecting him with the right people and launching him on a journey across the United States to compete in games, travel, and meet incredible people—including former *Survivor* contestants. Fueled by inspiration and connection, Chris thrives at the intersection of competition and community. When he's not scheming his next move, he enjoys traveling, pop culture, drag queens, and pop music.

Danny Vogwill (they/them), hails from the windy city of Chicago, IL. They have been a part of the Live Reality Game community since 2022, but their roots go much deeper. Back in 2012, Danny was hosting their own games inspired by this community and their favorite TV shows, producing 15 seasons of *Survivor*-style games and 5 seasons of *Big Brother*-style games.

The Live Reality Games you may recognize Danny from include *Survive, The Golden Gates, Surviving Bloomington, Weekender,* and more, just missing out on the crown time after time. Danny brings an undeniable charm, uniqueness, and personality to every game they are in! The confessional is their secret weapon, drawing the audience into the game and making them laugh. They compete in these games for the little boy who used to get made fun of for wearing a buff to school, mocked for being skinny and hid their queerness in defense.

Outside of these games, Danny is a model and luxury sales manager with a passion for fashion. They shop exclusively second-hand and up-cycle most things in their wardrobe as they express themselves through

---

* To learn more about Carlos, you can find him on Facebook and Instagram.

clothes. Whether on the street or in the game, Danny brings as many accessories as they can because style, like strategy, is always part of the story!

Da'Vontae Randolph is a 28 year old first-generation college graduate from Indiana University who now lives in Indianapolis, Indiana after growing up in Marion, Indiana. Glued to reality competition television from adolescence, he fell in love with *Survivor* at the age of eleven - a fascination he has never let go. Since then he has turned fandom into experience, competing in nine LRGs with one victory and three second-place finishes under his belt, and having always made the merge. His passion for playing LRGs extends beyond playing, as every year he works production for Surviving Bloomington, his first LRG, helping with casting and game logistics.

Passionate, energetic, and personable, he thrives in environments that blend strategy, creativity, and connection. Outside of the LRG community he enjoys being outdoors, watching movies, playing with his cat Luna, and spending quality time with his family and friends. He also works on the LRG Documentary and serves as the Editor of its companion blog series, *"The Fire We Carry"*—projects he finds both rewarding and meaningful. He is driven by big ideas and bigger dreams, especially the goal of one day playing *Survivor*. But in the meantime he loves to be a voice for the BIPOC and LGBTQ+ communities; both of which he is a part of. At heart, he is someone who believes that LRGs can tell stories — and that the best ones are fueled by people bold enough to play.

Daniel Suckow is currently a full time student at Brigham Young University in Utah, planning to graduate as a teacher in secondary education in April 2026. He grew up in a small town in Alaska, moving to Utah for school in 2020. As a relatively inexperienced LRG player, he was interested to join for an opportunity to attempt to experience what he sees on TV. In the future, he would like to play more *Survivor*-based LRG games if given the opportunity, especially as a way to meet more people with this interest. Outside of the game, Daniel loves Jesus, music, hockey, and spending time with friends.

Dejuan Watts grew up in Philadelphia with dreams of making it out of the city. He found Live Reality Games to be the perfect catalyst to start his journey, and has traveled across the country learning and growing with every new adventure.

Both he and his partner, Michael Bridenhagen, are continually impressed by how the community has grown and evolved since 2015. He is appreciative of the experiences, hosts, players, and friends (who in many cases became family) he met along the way.

Although Dejuan is currently "retired"... *never say never.*

Eric Eldredge is an ex-video producer-turned-game designer who is singularly focused on unscripted competition television shows.

Erin O'Mara Kunz is a Social Psychologist and Professor, currently living in Dayton Ohio with her husband and their daughter. Erin grew up in Long Island, NY, and was in college at Quinnipiac University when *Survivor* first aired. An instant fan, Erin never anticipated what her future would hold regarding *Survivor*, 20+ years later. Having spent most of *Survivor*'s 50 seasons feeling like the only fan she knew (aside from her mom), she didn't become aware of the LRG world until 2023 after her research on *Survivor* brought members of the LRG community into her life.

As a former D-1 women's lacrosse player, Erin was up for the physical challenge of *Survivor-style* LRGs especially since, for most fans, these games are the closest they'll get to playing "the real thing." Since then, she has embraced and immersed herself in the incredible LRG community, and made so many incredible friendships with people she may have never met otherwise. Erin has mostly stuck to *Survivor*-style and *Traitors*-style LRGs, but has begun branching out into *The Mole*-style LRGs and hopes to continue to improve her game.

Frances Diederich *

Jacob Burklow-Rogers grew up traversing the woods, creeks & ravines

---

* To learn more about Frances or her LRG, please follow @lrg_casting instagram

of Indiana, building forts, wading through rivers and hunting for hidden treasures. Family nights were spent with his mom, dad, and three siblings watching *Survivor* on the couch, never realizing how deeply it would shape his life. Inspiration sparked watching fellow Hoosier Rupert Boneham. Jacob carried that spark from backyard adventures to real-life games, finding in the LRG community not just competition, but connection.

For Jacob, the fire of the game is more than strategy, it's self-discovery. Through challenge, reflection, and friendship, he's learned that the greatest treasure isn't winning, but becoming. He believes when you push your limits and embrace the discomfort, you don't just play the game, you find your truest self.

Jacob won his season of *Survivor Indiana*. He also played in *Outlast* season 2, *Surviving Bloomington* season 7 and *Survivor Legends* which you can find on *Youtube*.

Jaymes Lanoye is a living story of one man's fight to find space for himself in the world. A story of growing up too early, learning through trial and error, and yet finding hope in what the future could look like for someone who started with such humble beginnings. Jaymes is a kindness warrior in one aspect, and a take no bullshit gladiator in another. Jaymes has made it his life goal to travel as far and wide as he can, touching as many lives as he gets the opportunity to, and experiencing every sort of life altering adrenaline rush that he comes across. In the face of adversity, poverty, homelessness, neglect, and learning to find his place, his story is that of the ruthless underdog. The kid that won't quit. A savage. A warrior. A survivor.

John Vataha and his wife Linda live in Florida. They have 3 adult children and 1 grandson. John is an entrepreneur and has run his own consulting business for more than 25 years. He loves the outdoors including hiking, biking and exploring nature. The beach is a happy place for him where he can relax and recharge to take on the next challenge. He is very involved in leadership in his church and enjoys leading the Bible study group that meets at his house. John always looks forward to every opportunity to get together with *Survival Challenge* alumni who have become friends and extended family.

Kadie Yannone is a 37 year old mom from Boston, MA. Kadie grew up in a small town, Dover MA and is the oldest of 4 siblings, twins Steph and Jordana and brother Jordan Greenfield. She grew up doing theater at her parents theater group, *Open Fields*. Kadie's parents supported her love of the arts and her competitive drive as a gymnast throughout her childhood. After graduating from Connecticut College, Kadie auditioned for the show *Rent* and was cast as Mimi and her now husband, Allen was Roger. Kadie and Allen's love for theater sparked their flame and after starting a family, LRGs became their new theater. Kadie has two sons, Quinn 7 and Theo 3. Kadie loves nothing more than her two boys and her family.

Being away from her kids is the hardest part of playing these games, but it is the competitive vacation she needs. Kadie played her first LRG, *Survival Challenge* in 2021, followed by *Can You Survive's* first season in 2021. Kadie has also played *Survivor Angelica, CYS Blood VS Water, Surfifer Prom, The Challenge Great Lakes* and *Survival Challenge's* final season, *Unfinished Business*. In 2025, Kadie and her husband Allen decided to team up with CYS's Brandon Clark to open *The Reality Retreat* in Newport Maine. This location is the new permanent home for CYS and is also hosting competitive reality vacations away for anyone interested. Kadie is beyond grateful for all of the relationships she has fostered in the woods. The LRG family has brought Kadie new friends she considers family, memories that will last forever and has kept her theater loving self alive.

Kc Winnecke has been an avid fan of *Survivor* since he was a child. When he moved to Bloomington in 2016, he started volunteering at Shalom Community Center, where he became passionate about helping homeless people, and was taking human service classes locally through Ivy Tech.

In 2018, he created Surviving Bloomington, a local event inspired by the show *Survivor*, a reality TV show where a group of strangers must provide food, fire and shelter for themselves while in an isolated location. They compete in challenges for rewards and immunity from elimination and are voted out by fellow contestants until one remains and wins the grand prize. *Surviving Bloomington* was designed to raise awareness of and support for people experiencing homelessness in Bloomington.

Keenan Lucas' fascination with *Survivor* since his youth led him to play his very first LRG in July of 2020 and *Survivor Blue Ridge* in 2025. With his enthusiasm and competitive drive, he's now played a total of four games, the latter three not being in his home country. The games have allowed him to make many of the friends he has today with hopes the connections last a lifetime.

Between playing, his two friends decided to ask him to be a part of starting up *Surviving Canada*, a charity based game in Vancouver. He said yes, and took on the hosting role; a role he enjoys much more than playing. Outside of his LRG obsession, Lucas enjoys outdoor adventures, skiing, cooking, going to the beach (weather permitted), and spending quality time with close friends and family. Currently single, Lucas resides in Port Moody, Canada with his two roommates, and works at the Port of Vancouver. Work and life depending, he desires to host again, and just maybe... come back to the LRG world as a player.

Mae Messersmith has been a Reality Competition fan from the young age of 8 years old. Her family would watch *The Amazing Race* from different places and call each other over the landline after the episodes were over to discuss the challenges, locations and favorites! It was these types of shows and the personalities shown on the screen that made Mae feel like she would belong in the world.

Following this passion led her into the world of Online Reality Games where she would make lifelong friends from across the world— one of which (King Lance Richards) would invite her into the world of LRGs! Starting with season 1 of *Surviving Maine* to prepare her for an 8 day *Survivor* game; Mae has since played and/or produced over 30 different LRGs including formats like: *Big Brother, Survivor, Traitors, The Mole, The Challenge* and original formats like *Gold Gates*! Mae strives to make the LRG community a welcome place that fosters friendships, goals and sportsmanship.

Melanie Bartlett entered the LRG community after hearing about a one day game in her city, *Survivor Philadelphia* in 2019. Although she was out at her first tribal council, she stayed to watch the events unfold and was immediately hooked on LRGs. She went on to play many games across the country, for over 39 days of *Survivor*-style LRGs, including several of the longest and most "deprivation" style games, a Blood vs. Water game with her mother, and she has earned the sole survivor title. Melanie has also volunteered on production for many games and, on occasion, brings her daughter to help, too.

Melanie's biggest contribution to the community is through the creation and running of the **@lrg_casting instagram** account that connects people interested in playing games with hosts who are casting. Countless players have discovered the LRG community through this page, and Melanie is always available to assist when people have questions. Melanie has also been part of the team to build a central LRG website, and is on the Table for the LRG Documentary. When she isn't volunteering as an LRG community organizer, she may be off enjoying her other hobbies, including skateboarding and pole dancing. She also has many years of experience as a social justice activist and currently works at the School District of Philadelphia.

Mira Hall is a 28 year old Ryan White case manager with a passion for advocacy that's rivaled only by her determination to be an agent of chaos. Since having this interview Mira has gone on to compete in 12 games total and finally got her first victory, *Frances Franchise Season 2*. Mira walked away with the crown and the 500$ prize pot; which she used to pay her law school seat deposit. That's right she's in law school part time in the evenings now, just having completed her first semester in the winter of 2025. Mira aims to become a civil rights attorney to help defend those who are the most marginalized in her community. Mira also has been cultivating her social media persona as a plus size fashion nano influencer (that's a real term check it out!) showcasing how different styles look on plus size bodies and breaking barriers that society has around what a plus size woman can wear.

Mira continues being open with her diagnoses as an autistic adult and has been featured on Tabitha Ziegler's podcast *"Staring Down the Storm: Autism Advocacy in America"*. Mira will make her return to *Surviving Bloomington* in season 8 of the series after having to leave while filming season 7 due to medical complications and cannot wait for the world to see the story arc she ends up on this season. Will she hold onto her title of Villain Queen of LRGs, or will we see her turning over a new life and diving head first into the hero pool? Mira encourages anyone who may have questions about doing a game to reach out to her, or if they have questions about any of the other aspects of her life (queer sports captain, plus size fashion, women with AuDHD). She hopes you find this chapter as beautiful and moving as she did.

Naomi C. has been the executive producer of *Survivor New York* for 7 seasons. She first began her descent into *Survivor* obsession producing a live *Survivor* comedy show in New York City. She has been privileged to travel the country and help friends produce incredible LRGs, each with a unique place in her heart.

Naomi also served on the Live Reality Games podcast executive board for two years, producing coverage of iconic LRG seasons and hours of content exploring the players and their journeys through games. She won exactly one LRG, and has since retired.

Nikki Neises, 36, is an LRG player and host. She is from McHenry Illinois and this is where she has hosted her game, *Survive*. Outside of LRGs Nikki is a healthcare AI sales representative. She has three cats, all foster fails. Her and her cats live with her boyfriend Baker whom she met playing pickleball. They are working towards building a family together. Nikki loves all games related to social strategy. You will find Nikki hosting board game nights, playing video games with her cousin, competing in LRGs and watching the latest strategic reality television competition. She rarely gets angry and tends to stay positive in stressful situations which has helped her achieve some of her life goals like hosting an LRG and maintaining a successful career.

Rachel Rowe Once upon a time, Rachel stepped into the deep woods of Bloomington, Indiana and delighted in the friendships and stories told as they walked through the mud and slept under the stars. Her body was pushed, her mind was stretched--the adventure forced her to reconcile her own worth and her doubts. She left the game with gratitude and a strength she still walks in today. When not in the woods, she's curled up on the couch reading a book, often with a little one snuggled in by her. Her family shares a love for *Survivor* and LRGs. You can often find her children hiding fake idols or giving their mom new challenges to train for an upcoming game. She has played in several LRGs including *Columbus Survivor All-Stars*, *The Mole Ohio*, *Surviving Bloomington*, and *Survivor Indiana*. She helps co-host *The Mole* Ohio. She invites you to be a part of the next chapter of LRGs-- what story will you tell? She cannot wait to hear it.

Renzo Santos was born and raised in Manila, Philippines, shaped by his parents' humble beginnings in the northern provinces of the country. Growing up was not easy, and from an early age he carried a deep curiosity about who he was, where he belonged, and how people find their way in the world. Reality shows like *Survivor* and *The Amazing Race* became a source of comfort and escape, offering him a window into resilience and possibility while he navigated a life that looked simple on the outside but felt complex within.

He eventually settled in San Francisco, California, where he works for a nonprofit public media organization as a Finance Manager. Moving to San Francisco in 2017 was a pivotal moment, immersing him in a richly diverse, community-oriented environment that helped him better understand his identity and values. Supporting mission-driven organizations has since become a major part of his DNA.

His introduction to LRGs began during the pandemic, after watching former *Survivor* players compete in online reality games. Within a week he joined one himself, and ORGs quickly became a meaningful part of his pandemic life. After lockdown, he played his first LRG while wearing a full arm cast from a wrist he had broken just two weeks earlier, a reflection of his bold and competitive spirit. A lifelong fan of game theory and tactics, he credits Microsoft Excel as his first love and believes that being good at math may have quietly helped him survive a difficult childhood. Outside of games and spreadsheets, he finds joy in movies, yoga, staying active, and coffee, which he treats with the same seriousness as strategy and spreadsheets.

Sandra Diaz-Twine the *Queen of Survivor*, lives in Fayetteville, North Carolina. She is often invited by fans and ORGs to participate in their games. While Sandra hasn't always been able to say yes, if she is available, she will always participate. Her most recent venture was playing in the *North Myrtle Beach Celebrity Survivor Challenge, Season 1* — and returning Season II as a volunteer. Other games include *Vanquish Presents the Traitors. Flight or Flight Mini, Fans vs. Favorites Vanquish, and Survival Challenge Maine.* She is always been excited to play and hates when she is voted out amongst the first.

Shaw Ashley first became familiar with the *Survivor* community in 2018 during the airing of *Season 37: David vs. Goliath*. While home sick from school, he was browsing through channels on the television where he came across a live episode of Season 37. He became infatuated with the show and went back and watched seasons 1-36 multiple times. Throughout his teen years he was involved in a number of organizations in his hometown of North Myrtle Beach, South Carolina, where he worked with children.

During the height of COVID-19 in 2020, he saw a need to get kids back outdoors as most summer camp programs were closed due to the pandemic. In 2021, as a Freshman in high school, he launched the "NMB Jr. Survivor Camp", a Christian-based summer camp based off of the hit CBS show, *Survivor*. The first year of camp was a success. In 2022, he launched the *"NMB Celebrity Survivor Challenge"*, a weekend-long LRG that featured local celebrities in the area with contestants from the real show! The live game was a fundraiser which benefited the kids camp.

Season 1 featured 12 local celebrities and two celebrities from the show; Sandra Diaz-Twine (*Survivor*s 7, 20, 34, 39 & 40) & Chris Underwood (Winner of *Survivor* 38). In 2023, Season 2 of the LRG was aired with 12 local celebrities alongside *Survivor* contestants; Jonny

Fairplay (*Survivor* 7 & 16), Crystal Cox (*Survivor* 17) & Marya Sherron (*Survivor* 42). After two amazing seasons alongside his Co-Host, Meredith Chandler, the LRG came to an end. The kids summer camp lasted through summer 2024, which marked the final year of camp. After graduating from high school in 2024 he needed to take a break and focus on the next chapter in life.

Shaw currently studies Elementary Education with double-minors in Athletic Leadership & Political Science at Clemson University. Since attending Clemson, he has launched the "Clemson *Survivor* Fans" organization which hosts weekly *Survivor* watch parties. He hopes to host the first on-campus LRG in Spring 2026. Since becoming an adult he has competed in his first LRG, in December 2025, with many more applications in. The *Survivor* and LRG community has given him so much at a young age, he hopes he can continue to give back in his adult life.

Stephen Stewart, when not working as an assistant accounting professor, is a connoisseur of all things LRG related. He loves supporting the community by participating, watching, and podcasting about different LRGs. He currently is one of the podcasters for the LRG Podcast, where he covers games such as *Surviving Bloomington* and *Surviving Reelfoot* as well as interviews various game creators. He also has been a major contributor to developing the LRG wiki. He has competed in nine different LRGs, enjoying *Survivor-style* and *Mole-style* games the most. And while *Survivor* is his passion, he apparently is much better at *The Mole*-style games. He hopes to continue to be a part of this community and has loved watching it flourish over the past decade.

Zach Fifer lives in Denver, Colorado with his incredible miniature Goldendoodle, Heath, and a philosophy inherited from his Indiana roots: always play through life with joy. An actor and fine-dining server by trade, Zach is also the visionary creator and host of *SurFifer*. Through his company Camp Reality, he transforms the "everyday" into the extraordinary by bringing the immersive thrill of Live Reality Games to backyards and woods alike. Whether in-person or online, Zach's mission is to make high-stakes gaming accessible to everyone.

Between producing games in hubs like NYC and LA, he finds his own fun in the theatre, the great outdoors, and the ever-growing *SurFifer* community. He also continues to stoke the flames of his passion as a founding Table member and executive team member for the LRG Documentary, directed by Marya Sherron. Having lived across the country, Zach thrives on connecting brilliant souls and building spaces where people can play together. Even when he isn't busy producing—which isn't very often—he is constantly dreaming up new ways to innovate. For Zach, the future holds more games, more memories, and always a few surprises up his sleeve.

Acknowledgments

This book concludes where so much of my life does... *with gratitude.*

David... thank you for your unending support of my passions, my storytelling, and the many seasons where an idea takes hold and refuses to let go. You have stood beside me through long hours, shifting focus, and the quiet demands of creative work. Your steadiness has made space for me to chase what calls me... and to see it through to completion.

My experience at *Surviving Bloomington* Season 7 was the origin of an ember that would not die. I left deeply inspired, challenged, curious, and changed. There was a knowing I could not shake... that the LRG community was special, and that its story deserved to be explored with care. What began there has grown into both this book and what would become our documentary project. For that beginning... I am deeply grateful.

To the OG LRG Doc Developmental Table... *Kc, Zach, Melanie, Da'Vontae, Naomi, Allen, Nikki, Danny, Eric...* and our recent additions, *Alyson, Hieu, and Rachael...* while much of our shared work has centered on the documentary, your presence has shaped this book in ways both seen and unseen. Your loyalty, your trust in my leadership, and your willingness to build something together have humbled me. You have challenged me to be better... to lead with clarity and care... and, most importantly, to finish what I start.

To the contributors... you said yes to a conversation without fully knowing what it would become. You trusted me with your stories, your reflections, and your honesty. Across more than sixty hours of interviews, I listened, transcribed, revisited, and searched for meaning—not only in what was said, but in what lingered beneath the surface. The process was all-consuming and deeply personal. It was an honor to witness your wisdom, your authenticity, and the fullness of your humanity. You gave this book its heartbeat.

To those I hoped to interview but could not quite make happen... *Drew, Taylor, Mackenzi, Stacie, T.J., Alex, Rachael...* your presence in this community, and the stories I know you carry, are part of what continues to call me forward. You are a meaningful part of why I have committed to *LRG Nation: Book II.*

A special thank you to *John Vataha*, who stepped into the role of *Editor* with thoughtful care, helpful insight, and encouraging feedback. Your willingness to serve in this capacity reflects not only your skill, but your love for this community. *To Erin...* thank you for saying yes without hesitation when I asked you to write the Foreword. Your voice brings depth and grounding to this work, and I am honored to have it open these pages.

In the end, this is a printed collection of stories... but it has never been only that. It is a record of connection, of courage, and of the quiet, complicated ways people come to know themselves and one another. More than anything, it is a reflection of the people who chose to show up, to be honest, and to be seen. Thank you for trusting me with what matters to you.

Huge Thank You to *Jacob Burklow-Rogers* for graciously jumping on board to do a "Final-Final" read through for necessary edits!

ABOUT THE AUTHOR

Marya Patrice Sherron is a writer, publisher, and storyteller devoted to capturing the moments that reveal who we are beneath the surface. Her work explores the intersection of identity, pressure, and belonging... the spaces where people are stretched, where certainty falls away, and authnticity begins to emerge.

As the founder of KĪ Productions, a boutique publishing company, Marya partners with individuals and organizations to bring meaningful stories into the world with care, clarity, and intention. Her work is deeply relational... shaped by conversation, trust, and a commitment to preserving the integrity of each voice. She does not write to speak for others, but to create space where people can be fully seen and heard.

That commitment finds one of its clearest expressions through *Neurodiversity Press*... a pioneering imprint dedicated to elevating neurodivergent voices and stories from within the disability community. Here, Marya works alongside individuals whose experiences have too often been overlooked, creating space not only for their stories to be told, but for them to be held with dignity, depth, and truth. It is work rooted in advocacy and reverence... a belief that when voices long pushed to the margins are brought forward with care, they do more than inform... they expand how we see, how we listen, and how we belong to one another.

LRG Nation began not as a project, but as a moment of recognition. What first appeared to be a community centered around gameplay revealed itself to be something far more complex... a landscape where people step into uncertainty, navigate connection, confront perception, and, in many cases, encounter themselves in ways they had not before.

Over the course of more than 70 hours of interviews, Marya sat with players, creators, and community members, listening not for strategy or outcome, but for what lived underneath. What surfaced were stories of courage, grief, resilience, identity, and transformation... stories that extend far beyond the boundaries of any game.

This book is not an explanation of Live Reality Games. It is a reflection of the people within them... and of the quiet, often unseen ways we are shaped when we choose to step into something uncertain.

Marya's work continues to be guided by a simple but enduring belief... that when we slow down long enough to truly listen, we begin to recognize one another more fully... and, in doing so, we come closer to understanding ourselves.

Marya Patrice Sherron | *The Dancing Pen*

lrgnation.com
Kiproductionsandpublishing.com
@KI.Productions928